Art Education

A Canadian Perspective

Art Education

A Canadian Perspective

Roger Clark
The University of Western Ontario

Ontario Society for Education through Art
Toronto

Cover: *Interplanetary Voyage* by John MacGregor (1967).
Purchase, Centennial Grant from the Province of Ontario, 1967.
Reproduced with permission from the artist and The McIntosh Gallery, The University of Western Ontario, London, Ontario.

Canadian Cataloguing in Publication Data

Clark, Roger Allen, 1953-
  Art education: a Canadian perspective

Includes bibliographic references and index.
ISBN 0-9698237-0-3

1. Art - Study and teaching (Elementary). 2. Art - Study and teaching (Secondary). I. Ontario Society for Education through Art. II. Title.

N365.C2C5 1994   707'.1'2   C94-931019-0

Published by the Ontario Society for Education through Art.
Printed and bound in Canada by The Aylmer Express Ltd., Aylmer, Ontario.

■ Dedications

Richard Courtney

Professor Emeritus
Department of Curriculum
Ontario Institute for Studies in Education

Dr. Kishio Matoba

Professor Emeritus
Department of Art Education
State University College at Buffalo

A.D. (Dan) Logan

Professor Emeritus
Faculty of Education
The University of Western Ontario

Carman F. Harrison

(Retired)
Department Head, Art
Delta Secondary School, Hamilton (Ontario)

■ Contents

■ Figures

■ Introduction

This book has been written primarily to address the needs of generalist elementary educators, for whom art is often a mysterious and personally intimidating part of professional practice. My goal has been to provide courage to those colleagues, for art education can be a rewarding experience for students and teachers alike.

The book is divided into four chapters that situate art within the context of contemporary school curricula. Chapter 1 provides an historical overview of art, from its emergence as drawing to its present dual function as both discipline and methodology. Chapter 2 presents a variety of issues related to art's search for unity, integration, and identity. Chapter 3 delves into the nature of creativity, aesthetics, and artistic disclosure. Chapter 4 offers practical insights into the planning, implementation, and assessment of art activities.

The successful inculcation of art is within the grasp of any educator who integrates the unique aspects of artistic activity with the fundamental elements of effective teaching.

Roger Clark

Acknowledgement

I would like to take this opportunity to thank

Peder & Valerie Nielsen

for their constant encouragement
and technical assistance.

1   Art as an Emergent School Subject

> What if imagination and art are not frosting at all, but
> the fountainhead of human experience? What if our
> logic and science derive from art forms and are
> fundamentally dependent on them rather than art being
> merely a decoration for our work when science and logic
> have produced it? (p. 150)
>
> Rollo May (1975)
> *The Courage to Create*

It takes courage to create. According to Rollo May, there are many kinds of courage: physical, moral, and social. But **the most important of all is the courage to create, which requires an encounter between the subjective self and the objective world**.[1]

This book is all about such encounters, and how teachers can cultivate the courage to create. We will be exploring encounters that occur when teachers and students use studio activities to engage self in *artistic disclosure* (education *in* art), and those which occur when they use studio activities to engage self in *generic development* (education *through* art).

During such pedagogic encounters, teaching itself becomes a creative act needing courage. And just as the courage to create required an encounter between self and world, **teaching requires an encounter between educator and practice**. This book has been written to provide courage to educators during their encounters with an often intimidating area of professional practice: art education.

Teaching art can induce anxiety among even the most courageous of educators; therefore, the suggestions in this book should be considered analogous to the advice dispensed to the ancient Greeks by Apollo's priestesses at Delphi:

> The counsels of Delphi were not advice in the strict sense,
> but rather were stimulants to the individual and to the
> group to look inward, to consult their own intuition and
> wisdom. The oracles put the problem in a new context so
> that it could be seen in a different way, a way in which new
> and as yet unimagined possibilities would become evident.
> (May, 1975, p. 127)

1.1   Divergent roots of art education

In order to fully appreciate the unique role played by art within professional practice, educators need to be acquainted with the historical emergence of art education. To accomplish this task we will be looking at the emergence of art in the province of Ontario,[2] other Canadian provinces such as British Columbia[3] and Nova Scotia,[4] and sister dominions within the 19th century British empire, including those as diverse as New Zealand and South Africa.[5]

The introduction of mechanical drawing curricula

Art, as we know it today, did not exist in the curricula of 19th century common[6] schools; rather, **the forerunner of contemporary art education was** *drawing.* **These early drawing courses were designed to train draughtsmen in mechanical illustration.** Art education historians frequently credit Massachusetts superintendent of education Horace Mann for the introduction of compulsory drawing instruction in various North American jurisdictions.[7] Canadians, however, may take pride in the fact that drawing was made part of *common education* throughout British North America almost a quarter century **prior** to the *Massachusetts Act of 1870.*

The gradual evolution of post-common school curricula, however, placed art education in a decidedly "secondary" role. This development could have been predicted since, even though all were compulsory, subjects within common education were usually given unequal status. In Ontario, Egerton Ryerson divided common school subjects into *cardinal, required,* and *other.*

> The three cardinal subjects--Reading (including Spelling), Writing and Arithmetic--constitute primary knowledge and elements of intellectual power. In addition, two required subjects, Grammar (acquainting us with the language we speak) and Geography (exhibiting to us the world we inhabit), teach how to employ the cardinal subjects in the most useful manner and in relation to the common interests of life. As part of nineteenth century general education, Drawing is placed in the category of "other" subjects: a position which is similar to, yet conceptually broader than, its limited placement in twentieth century comprehensive art courses. (Martin, 1993, p. 47)

The seeds for inferior status having been sown within common school curricula, drawing became an optional subject within the forerunner of secondary schooling, *superior education.* Superior education consisted of studies that provided future civic leaders with a background in the liberal arts; thus, the foundation of superior education was a knowledge of Greek and Roman culture. To this core was added mathematics, natural philosophy, history, geography, English grammar and composition, and in many schools, practical subjects such as bookkeeping, drawing, and commercial arithmetic.[8]

Thus, the origins of two of contemporary art education's enduring albatrosses have been identified: its designation as one of the *other* subjects within Ryerson's common education, and its status as an *optional* subject within boy's superior education. A third lingering curricular stereotype, the notion that art is a *girl's* subject, can be traced to the introduction of superior education for girls:

> A superior education for girls differed from that of boys in some fundamental ways. Girls too would learn the three Rs and the more advanced parts of an English education, studying many of the same subjects as boys. But along with the "solid" or academic subjects, they would also take a variety of "ornamental" studies that might include fancy needlework, drawing and painting, instrumental music, dancing, French, and other modern languages. (Gidney & Millar, 1990, p. 15)

The development of a separate superior education for girls, usually referred to as the *accomplishments curriculum*, signalled the birth of modern art education, as well as instrumental music and dance. Classes in drawing and painting for girls, as opposed to instruction in geometrical drawing for boys, were defended on both vocational and pedagogic grounds:

> It was almost universally assumed that beyond the limits of a common English education, the schooling of boys and girls would be different, and that in turn reflected not just the separate spheres that they might occupy in adult life, but the differences in their mental propensities and capacities. (Gidney & Millar, 1990, p. 247)

Similar art curricula evolved throughout the English-speaking world, including the United States.[9] The global reach of the 19th century British empire resulted in the *South Kensington model of art education* taking hold not only in Canada, but in other dominions within our imperial family, such as New Zealand and South Africa:[10]

> Beginning after the Great Exhibition in London in 1851, a new government Department of Practical Art, subsequently incorporated into the Department of Science and Art at South Kensington, initiated in Britain a system of state-aided and controlled art schools and examinations, supposedly concentrating on efficiency and consistent goals. ...The Department of Science and Art not only supervised the teaching of art throughout Britain, it also examined

generalist teachers in art and trained art masters. The essence of what has been called "The South Kensington System" lay in the manner in which teachers and children were taught to exactly delineate plane and then solid geometrical forms. Only at an advanced stage was there any reference to nature. This is the system that was exported to New Zealand. (Chalmers, 1990, pp. 71-72)

The international reach of the South Kensington model helps explain why some essential features of 19th century drawing curricula have endured to the present day.[11] The South Kensington model also firmly entrenched the role of applied art within vocational schools, whether at the secondary or post-secondary level:

Many of these schools shared a common purpose: to sharpen the graphic skills of working class industrial designers, to provide the well-to-do with instruction in the decorative arts, and to train drawing teachers for the private and public schools. (Soucy, 1989, p. 24)

In Ontario flagship art departments were frequently housed within large technical secondary schools until World War II, such as those in Toronto (Central, Danforth, Northern, and Western), Hamilton (Central), and London (Beal).[12]   Although enrolment within vocational art programmes has steadily declined in most of these historic technical schools, vocational art education is still very much alive in Ontario, especially within the province's extensive system of post-secondary community colleges.

Today, showpiece art departments in Ontario are usually found within academic settings, such as collegiate institutes or schools for the arts.[13] This change in venue paralleled the gradual ascendency of academic art over vocational art, an ascendency not due to any inherent superiority of aesthetics over technology, but to changes within the structure of secondary education in Ontario.

The separation of academic art from vocational art

As previously discussed, the forerunner of modern secondary schooling was superior education which from its inception had two streams divided by gender. By the 1870s almost half of the students enroled in Ontario high schools were girls. Initially, the presence of female students did not affect the male-oriented curriculum since it was widely expected that separate facilities for girls would be built as soon as public finances allowed.[14]   Private wealth did manage to provide separate high school opportunities for girls, such as the *Burlington Ladies' Academy*, which offered an accomplishments-centred curriculum:

They gave, as one of their advocates put it, "a liberal education, embracing a knowledge of Music and the Fine

Arts." Few of their students, said another, took only academic subjects. "More than 90% carry side by side with the prescribed course a very liberal course in Music and Art. Many of them are also well advanced in Art studies, Drawing, Water Colours and Oil Painting." (Gidney & Millar, 1990, p. 295)

But, as is often the case with so many temporary situations, the housing of girls in public high schools lingered on. **When it became clear that the girls were unlikely to ever be removed to their own schools, efforts were made to merge the female-oriented accomplishments curriculum with the existing boys' programme.** Unfortunately, such efforts were singularly unsuccessful, primarily due to financial restraints. Although authorities responsible for public education never denigrated the value of subjects unique to the accomplishments curriculum, the public perception that art and music were peripheral subjects, costly to provide, and not amenable to standardized examination signalled the demise of the accomplishments curriculum, a lasting legacy for girls who were made "honorary boys."[15]

Clearly, the initial introduction of art into Ontario secondary schools was not an overwhelming success. Its present dominance over vocational art resulted from the inability of technical education to find a secure place within the emerging secondary curricula, for "the acquisition of marketable skills, divorced from mental culture, was not education but training, and belonged elsewhere."[16] The "elsewhere" meant that vocational art would be housed in separate technical schools, and art would find its home in the forerunner of composite secondary schools, *collegiate institutes*. Separated from its vocational sibling, drawing gained the subject title of art, in 1904. Thus, this child of the accomplishments curriculum became the dominant form of art education in Ontario simply because it was housed in collegiate institutes, which rapidly eclipsed technical schools in terms of student enrolment.

After World War II, Ontario began to replace its collegiate institutes with more egalitarian, *composite secondary schools*, a process which resulted in technical courses being taught alongside academic and commercial subjects. In many instances, this educational marriage was of the shotgun variety. Technical courses were frequently taught in separate wings of buildings, and schools often adopted the oxymoronic title of "collegiate and vocational institute". Such solitudes made the unification of vocational art and art imprudent; the imprudent turned to impossible when the Ontario Ministry of Education unilaterally gave art the new title of *visual arts* in the mid-1970s.

The development of art as a pedagogic methodology

Thus, vocational art evolved from boys' superior education, and academic art from the girls' accomplishments curriculum, but what happened to the mechanical drawing classes within common schools? As common schools evolved into what we know today as elementary schools, and as entry into the workforce gradually began to require a high school education, the vocational training rationale for elementary art was replaced by educational goals derived from the theories of John Dewey, Maria Montessori, and Jean Piaget. Previously, **drawing instruction had relied upon tedious copy exercises.** In the following passage, Donald Soucy describes the use of such *copy books* in Nova Scotia:

> Materials and personnel in the schools were generally insufficient to offer anything but drawing and picture study. Prang Drawing Books and the Augsburg drawing series were adopted in the province in the first years of this century and they continued to be used for decades. The student's task was to copy drawings found in the text. Some schools had class sets of the books. In other schools, teachers were expected to reproduce the drawings on the blackboard for students to copy. (Soucy, 1989, p. 39)

The shift away from similar copy books in Ontario had become pronounced by 1904, the year drawing was redesignated art:

> The 1904 curricular revisions in general must have been dramatic, at least in presentation, if not too immediately in effect. The intent probably reflected more interest on the part of leading educators in the new field of psychology. Certainly one objective shifted from mechanical drawing based on official copy books to some concern for "the aesthetic" (whatever that meant at the time!), and a broader range of activities and materials. Clay modelling, picture study, and correlation with History, Nature Study, Manual Training, and English Composition were given emphasis. (Blackwell, 1989, p. 26)

As with most educational reforms, the transformation of elementary school drawing instruction into art was not only gradual, but haphazard. By the 1920s, elementary art curricula in New Brunswick still relied upon the outmoded copy book, and the official art curriculum in British Columbia still reflected British models from the turn of the century.[17] Although drawing copy books were officially banned in Ontario by 1910, the historical legacy of drawing continues to affect art education even today in terms of studio projects that emphasize value scales, golden section proportion, and linear perspective.[18]

Early forms of elementary school art instruction emphasized ornamental design, a departure from the old copy books with their fixation upon geometric drawing. Typifying this new emphasis, the 1922 *Ontario Department of Education Examination for Lower School Art* contained the following questions:

Design and express in watercolours in a pleasing colour scheme, any one of the following:

■   A cube-shaped lantern with pyramidal top, the whole to be seven inches high. Finish the decoration of one side of the lantern (both top and side sections).

■   A rug pattern, five inches by eight inches, made up of a border and an interior of squares and rectangles divided and arranged in pleasing proportions.

■   A poster, seven inches by ten inches, illustrative of coasting, and lettered H.S. COASTING PARTY. (Blackwell, 1989, p. 25)

Again, it is important to understand that the development of art education in Ontario was mirrored in most English-speaking countries. For example, in 1924, British Columbia published *A Manual of Drawing and Design* for use in all provincial schools, a document which closely paralleled similar curricula in Ontario. Drawing from nature was given a central role and compositional design was emphasized.[19]

Neither drawing nor the old practice of copying disappeared entirely from elementary art instruction. Both were sometimes retained, albeit in reconceptualized formats. Bill Weston, Art Master at the Vancouver Normal School, was one of the three authors of the 1924 British Columbia *Manual*. Weston retained copying, but used it as a *pedagogic device*, believing that it would simultaneously nurture both creativity and studio skills. Thus, Weston's curricula employed copying to "stimulate a sense of the beautiful."[20]

Elementary school art instruction underwent a more radical transformation after World War II. Lowenfeld & Brittain espoused child-based art activities that complemented Jean Piaget's psychological model of cognitive development, Maria Montessori's pedagogic model of auto-education, and John Dewey's curricular model of active learning.

Although each of these educational models stressed the value of providing opportunities for the manipulation of artistic media, it is important to note that such opportunities were fundamentally valued for their ability to be *instrumental* in the achievement of *generic educational goals*, rather than for their ability to develop art skills per se. Over time, **elementary art emerged as a cross-disciplinary pedagogic methodology, rather than a separate school subject**:

By the late 1940s, Gaitksell (1949) notes that the main purposes of teaching art in the state-supported schools are to assist people to develop to the full extent of their needs and capacities, and to become useful, valued, and co-operative members of their social group. Broader aims relating to responsibility toward the community, group co-operation, emotional stability, efficient methods of thinking, good taste, discrimination, leisure-time activities, and expression are advanced as being different from and more important than the former training of hand and eye. (Martin, 1993, pp. 53-54)

Art-as-methodology found an articulate proponent in Herbert Read, whose text *Education Through Art* provided both a theory and a name for the emerging movement. Thus, **through the efforts of Lowenfeld, Read, and Gaitskell elementary art education completed its evolution from mechanical drawing to pedagogic methodology**:

During the 1950s and early 1960s, Read's textbook, *Education Through Art* (1943), Lowenfeld's textbook, *Creative and Mental Growth* (1947), and Gaitskell's textbook, *Children and Their Art* (1958), were regarded as three of the most significant art education textbooks available. They denoted a child-centred era (or the romantic-expressionist stream as defined by Efland) of analyzing child art as a means of understanding and evaluating the intellectual and psychological development of children. The notion that creativity was best facilitated through studio experimentation became the central focus of many psychologists on behalf of art education. Lowenfeld's theoretical position explained the value of the child's innate abilities to create, the importance of the creative experience in order to develop the imagination of every child, and the justification of process over product. (Irwin, 1991b, p. 34)

1.2   Dominant influences in art education

Having highlighted the historical emergence of art as a school subject, **we will now turn our attention to changes in art that have been influenced by developments within the wider field of general education since 1900.** Our discussion will be guided by a chronological scheme, developed by United States art education historian Arthur Efland, **which traces two "discernible streams of influence that have coursed through the history of general education"**:

The first is a tradition of scientific rationalism; the other is the romantic-expressionist stream. By scientific rationalism I refer not to science proper, but to ideologies finding their warrant in science. By romantic-expressionist I refer to a loosely strung set of beliefs which place the artist in a vanguard position in social affairs. (Efland, 1990b, p. 117)

Efland's scheme is presented within *Figure 1a: Historical Patterns in General Education*.

Time Frame	Scientific-Rationalist Stream	Romantic-Expressive Stream
1900-1918	Social Efficiency	Romantic-Idealism
1929-1940	Instrumentalism	Creative Expression
1959-1965	Discipline-Centred	Counterculture
1965-1980	Accountability	Qualitative Inquiry
1980-	Excellence	Critical Theory

Figure 1a: Historical Patterns in General Education

(Efland, 1990b)

Social efficiency and romantic-idealism

At the turn of the century, educational theorists were still in the process of inventing the modern secondary school.[21] **The latter half of the 1800s had witnessed the demise of grammar schools, and the proliferation of practical subjects within the newly emergent secondary schools.** The ever-increasing diversity of secondary school curricula, however, forced educators to revisit the question of how society could determine the relative importance of individual school subjects.

In the United States, the National Education Association (NEA) established the *Committee of Ten on Secondary School Studies*, a panel of academics led by Harvard president Charles Eliot. The Committee of Ten recommended that all secondary school students study a common curriculum of nine subjects: Latin, Greek, English, modern languages, mathematics, physics and chemistry, biology, history and politics, and geography.[22] When deciding the relative importance of individual school subjects the Committee of Ten had relied upon a set of educational priorities developed by Herbert Spencer and outlined in his classic 1860 essay, "What Knowledge Is of Most Worth?":

- Those activities which directly minister to self-preservation;
- Those activities which, by securing the necessaries of life, indirectly minister to self-preservation;
- Those activities which have for their end the rearing and discipline of offspring;
- Those activities which are involved in the maintenance of proper social and political relations;
- Those miscellaneous activities which make up the leisure part of life, devoted to the gratification of the tastes and feelings. Spencer, 1860 (1911, p. 7)

Given such priorities, it was not surprising that the 1894 *Report* made few references to the arts, although drawing and music did retain elective status.

The Committee of Ten's curricular priorities reflected the scientific-rationalist notion of *social efficiency*. By World War I, school administrators in the United States had begun to consider themselves "managers in the business of education",[23] and efforts had been undertaken to make schools more "efficient" by eliminating subjects considered to be "non-productive". Early leaders in the emergent field of curriculum studies, such as Franklin Bobbitt, studied industrial settings in order to determine what adult life skills should be reflected within the goals and content of school curricula. In the new age of science, the most efficient use for art was the study of nature; as a result, **the 19th century Kensington preference for geometric drawing was replaced by exercises focused upon the direct observation of natural form**.

Although Efland's chronological scheme begins circa 1900, the goals of social efficiency did not first appear at the turn of the century. In fact, the Spencerian idea that the purpose of education was "to prepare the pupil for complete living" had been used 50 years earlier to justify the inclusion of drawing courses in school curricula throughout the English-speaking world.

The countervailing *romantic-idealistic* perspective within general education saw art as a way of "instilling in pupils a deep respect for social institutions and the moral ideals they espouse".[24] William Torrey Harris, superintendent of schools in St. Louis during the 1870s, believed that the arts could facilitate social control through the study of great civilizations from the past.[25] In the 19th century, romantic-idealistic notions had provided a foundation for the "accomplishments curriculum" designed for upper-class girls; in the 20th century, romantic-idealism facilitated the gradual transformation of mechanical drawing into art as we know it today.

Deweyan instrumentalism and creative expression

After the cataclysmic events of World War I, social changes in Western society prompted educators to institute major reforms in elementary schooling. One of the most important reforms undertaken involved the introduction of child-centred curricula. In 1919, the *Progressive Education Association* (PEA) was founded upon the following principles:

> the scientific study of child development, the conception of the teacher as a facilitator (rather than as a disciplinarian and lecturer), child interest as a primary motivator of learning, and cooperation between the school and home in meeting the needs of the child. (Longstreet & Shane, 1993, p. 24)

The progressive movement was also subjected to the opposing influences of scientific-rationalism and romantic-expressionism. The chief proponents of the former were Francis Parker, superintendent of schools in Quincy, Massachusetts from 1875 to 1883, and John Dewey who, in 1896, set up a laboratory school at the University of Chicago to test several educational hypotheses:

- that life itself...should furnish the ground of experience of education.
- that learning can be in large measure a by-product of social activity.
- that the main test of learning is the ability of individuals to meet new social situations with habits of considered action.
- that schooling, committed to cooperative effort on the one hand and scientific methods on the other, can be of beneficial influence on the course of social progress. (Efland, 1990b, p. 121)

Dewey believed that intelligence operated to produce instrumental knowledge, and he designed curricula to replace the 19th century approach to pedagogy which envisioned the learner as a passive vessel to be filled. *Instrumentalism* is a term that refers to instructional activities that are planned not so much for their own inherent value but for their ability to facilitate the acquisition of broader curricular objectives. The curriculum at Dewey's laboratory school included both fine and applied art activities, but they were taught within the context of child-centred social themes, rather than as discrete subject areas.

Progressive education was also influenced by the romantic-idealistic approach known as *creative expressionism*. Whereas Dewey's emphasis upon "the child-in-society" was rooted in science, creative expressionists such as Harold Rugg, Ann Schumaker, Florence Cane, Caroline Pratt, and Frank Cizek looked to the arts as models for curricular reform:

> The pupil is placed in an atmosphere conducive to self-expression in every aspect. Some will create with words, others with light. Some will express themselves through the body in dance; others will model, carve, shape their ideas in

plastic materials...But whatever the route, the medium, the materials - each one has some capacity for expression. (Rugg & Schumaker, 1928, p. 63)

The universality of creative expressionism and its relationship to psychological well-being were stressed in Viktor Lowenfeld's seminal text *Creative and Mental Growth.* Herbert Read extended these propositions in his book *Education Through Art,* by suggesting that child art could be instrumental in the maintenance of world peace.[26]

The child-centred strategies of the progressive movement replaced subject disciplines as the primary organizational core of elementary schooling. Art activities served this new approach very well, and elementary art education transformed itself from a subject discipline into a pedagogic methodology.

Discipline-centred curricula and counterculture

The progressive era ended as Cold War rivalries heated up in the late 1950s. Fears that Western schools were not sufficiently rigorous prompted university-based scholars to lobby for a return to *discipline-centred curricula.*[27] Science and mathematics were the earliest, and easiest, targets of such reform, but pressure was exerted upon all subject areas to prove that they, too, could be considered disciplines.

David Ecker's proposition that artistic activity was a form of "qualitative problem-solving" prompted Manuel Barkan to postulate that **the discipline of art consisted of three modes of [scientific] inquiry: studio, art history, and art criticism.** Thus the primary effects of discipline-centred trends upon art education during the 1960s were (a) a reduced emphasis upon studio activities, and (b) an increased attention to art history and art criticism.

The latter half of the decade witnessed the rise of a youth-inspired *counterculture.* Disillusioned by escalating levels of violence at home and abroad, many Americans began to lose their faith in scientific-rational institutions. Demands for personal liberation were heard everywhere, and especially in the halls of learning. Discipline-based curricula were perceived to be, at best irrelevant, and at worst, prime examples of domination by "the establishment". Proponents of counterculture reform often considered schools themselves to be problematic, and sought help for systemic change from community and political agencies.

Counterculture influences gave rise to the *arts-in-education* movement, in which the arts were taught collectively rather than as separate subjects. Typically, arts-in-education programmes stressed studio activities, relied heavily upon artists and art galleries as instructional resources, and promoted the arts as interdisciplinary pedagogic methodologies. Perhaps one of the best-known Canadian proponents of the arts-in-education movement is Richard Courtney, whose media-based model of learning is outlined in texts such as *The Dramatic Curriculum* (1980), *Re-play* (1982), and *Play, Drama & Thought* (1989).

Accountability and qualitative inquiry

During the 1970s, continual increases in the cost of public education, coupled with persistent doubts about the effectiveness of contemporary teaching methods, drew considerable attention to issues of educational *accountability*. Supporters of discipline-based approaches to teaching quickly took up the challenge by providing behavioural objectives upon which assessments could be confidently based.

A classic example of accountability-based curriculum, David Pratt's 1980 text *Curriculum: Design and Development* epitomized what has come to be known as the "positivist" view of educational theory. *Positivism* is based upon four theoretical assumptions:[28]

- By studying the fundamental laws that govern our physical world we are able to discover order and certainty.
- Given the fact of certainty, we can understand phenomena in terms of cause-and-effect.
- We are able to create methods of obtaining data that test out the certainty of reality.
- The results of such tests can be evaluated using techniques that allow for generalization to other situations.

Of course, not everyone shared the positivist penchant for preparing behavioural objectives. A group of theorists known as "reconceptualists"[29] argued in favour of curriculum planning based upon *qualitative inquiry*. For reconceptualists, instructional objectives could never adequately grasp the essence of the pedagogic "lived experience"[30] or the true nature of pedagogic practice. Notions of qualitative inquiry lie at the root of Michael Polyani's idea of "tacit knowledge" and Elliot Eisner's concept of "educational connoisseurship".

Excellence and critical theory

The publication of *A Nation at Risk* in 1983 by the National Commission on Excellence in Education sparked American fears of educational decay in the same way that Sputnik rattled nerves in the late 1950s, and the resulting calls for educational *excellence* paralleled earlier demands for school reform. Not surprisingly, the discipline-based art curriculum devised by Manuel Barkan and Elliot Eisner in the 1960s was again promoted as a model for excellence in art education; but this time around, *discipline-based art education* (DBAE) had an influential sponsor, the J. Paul Getty Trust. Through the Center for Education in the Arts, DBAE's four-part model of studio, art history, art criticism, and aesthetics was widely promoted throughout North America.

The increased attention paid to art history, art criticism, and aesthetics, provided fertile ground for the application of *critical theory* to art education. Vincent Lanier[31] was one of the first art educators to become involved with critical theory. His criticism of elitism within art education, to the exclusion of popular and folk arts, was subsequently joined by calls for:

- multicultural inclusiveness (Bracey, 1990; Chalmers, 1992; Clark, 1992c; Hamblen, 1986; MacGregor, 1979, 1990b);
- visual literacy (Lanier, 1982, 1990; Mansell, 1991; Matoba, 1985; Pearse, 1992c); and
- feminist perspectives (Collins & Sandell, 1984, 1987; Irwin, 1992c; Mansell, 1991; Snider, 1989).

1.3   Developing trends in art education

Confluent models of education

Efland's chronological scheme linking patterns in general education to trends in art education demonstrated the enduring strengths of *scientific-rationalism* and *romantic-expressionism*.   Clearly, neither represents a curricular fad; quite probably, each presents a curricular fact:

> In this century, the conflict in art education has been between those intent upon teaching the content of art and those seeing it as self-expression.   In the name of self-expression children were frequently left to their own devices and were denied access to knowledge that could enlighten their personal investigation of art.   And yet, in the insistence upon teaching art techniques, or the names and dates of art styles, or the elements and principles of design, one might easily lose touch with art as it enables human beings to realize their spirit and their destiny in the actions and products of the imagination. It remains to be seen how the drama of art education's future will be acted out. (Efland, 1990a, p. 263)

As we approach the start of a new century, **art educators are beginning to see these two streams of influence as halves of a unified whole. Education *in* art and education *through* art might not be discrete curricular models after all, but polar segments of a curricular continuum not yet fully sequenced.**   Similar views have been put forward in drama education, regarding the dichotomy in drama literature between theatre (education *in* drama) and dramatic play (education *through* drama).[32]

The notion that scientific-rational elements of curriculum theory (cognitive/discipline/product) and romantic-expressionist elements (affective/methodology/process) could be opposite sides of the same coin is not new. Such models were developed in the 1970s under the rubric of *confluent education*:[33]

> Confluent education stresses participation; it emphasizes power sharing, negotiations, and joint responsibility. It is essentially nonauthoritarian. It also stress the whole person and the integration of thinking, feeling, and acting. It centres on the relevance of subject matter in light of students' basic needs and lives. Throughout the curriculum, students are confronted with situations that make them realize that the development of self is a legitimate objective of learning. (Ornstein & Hunkins, 1993, p. 254)

Throughout this book we have will continue to talk about the need for such encounters between the subjective self and the objective world, and the participatory processes described by Allan Ornstein and Francis Hunkins parallel the nondirective teaching practices discussed in *Chapter 4: Art in Practice*.

Several developing trends in contemporary art education suggest that we have already begun the march "toward a harmonious confluence".[34] Indeed, the product/process concept of *artistic disclosure* is a pedagogic principle upon which a confluent model for art education could be constructed. For ease of discussion, we shall cluster developing trends that suggest a movement towards confluency into two groups:

- scientific-rationalist trends that are challenging traditional notions of education *through* art.
- romantic-expressive trends that are challenging traditional notions of education *in* art.

Scientific-rationalist trends

Art curricula within elementary schools have been premised upon the tenets of education through art ever since the rise of progressive education after World War I. Thus, **any attempt to reconcile education in art with education through art must deal with the enduring legacy of Viktor Lowenfeld, and the deeply-rooted principles of child art development.** These principles, known collectively as *developmentalism*, were promulgated in three classic texts: Lowenfeld's *Creative and Mental Growth*, Read's *Education Through Art*, and Gaitskell's *Children and Their Art*.

Developmentalism began with the advent of progressive education in the 1920s, a movement that accommodated both the instrumentalist approach of Dewey, and the creative expressionist emphases of Rugg and Schumaker. In the 1940s, Lowenfeld re-invigorated the field of elementary art education by merging the child-centred philosophy of progressive education with the newly emergent theories of *developmental psychology*. At the core of developmentalist orthodoxy was the belief that all children were natural-born artists; as such, they move innately through stages of artistic development.[35] Various models of developmentalism were subsequently proposed,[36] but each deviated only marginally from the stage model presented by Lowenfeld in *Creative and Mental Growth*.

The idea that all children "move innately through stages of artistic development", suggested that direct art instruction was unnecessary, an assumption that greatly increased its appeal to generalist elementary teachers. The extended notion that direct instruction was actually harmful to youthful expression was also readily accepted by many elementary practitioners.

As with most curricula designed for children, Lowenfeldian developmentalism works well in primary and junior grades. But children grow into teenagers, creatures that child art enthusiasts tend to see as big children with bad attitudes. The unwillingness of most preadolescents to engage in self-expressive activities is widely conceded by developmentalists, but usually ascribed to problems with the learner rather than with the pedagogic model.

Increasingly, however, the impotence of developmentalism in senior elementary school is being linked to problems within the model itself, and many art educators are suggesting that the decline in adolescent expression can be caused by an inadequate amount of *direct art instruction*:

> In short, expressions of frustration about their art is not a matter of young artists struggling to get out of society's straitjacket of conformity. More often than not, we are confronted by a young, astute intellect which knows lack of information when it is absent. All humans want to be competent. Praising children for art they deem incompetent is not encouraging to them. It is baffling. (Templeton, 1990, p. 34)

A substantial portion of most direct art instruction in senior elementary grades is heavily centred upon the acquisition of representational drawing skills. Recently, a study was undertaken to ascertain what kinds of drawing curricula would be best suited to the developmental needs of students aged nine to thirteen. Six current drawing programmes were analyzed for their ability to respond to the perceptual, psychosocial, and cognitive developmental needs of young students:

> For drawing programs to be effective, they must make sense to the learners. However, programs do not teach drawing; art educators do. None of the drawing programs analyzed would make sense or be considered worthwhile without considerable mediation by art teachers. Teacher

mediation should include the formulation of context-originated program goals that begin at learners' developmental levels, validate personal and social experiences, increase drawing competencies, and extend developmental dimensions while enriching understanding and appreciation of learners' own and other cultures' drawing systems and values. (Moody, 1992, pp. 45-46)

Moody's list of criteria for drawing programmes contrasts sharply with Lowenfeld's central preoccupation with creativity.

The idea that self-expression would inherently lead to original work produced the edict that "children should not copy anything."[37] The ban on copying was an early principle of developmentalism; however, the notion that copying was harmful to artistic growth originated at the turn of the century, during the transformation of mechanical drawing into art.[38]

This long-held edict against copying is still an official policy of the *Canadian Society for Education through Art* (CSEA).[39] In recent years, however, many art educators have come to the conclusion that this policy needs to be seriously reconsidered. Anna Kindler has emphasized the fact that children do not always set out to produce original material, and she has warned against the "worship of creativity". As well, Kindler has pointed out that **children do not use copying the same way that adults do; for many children, copying is a practical strategy that facilitates their movement away from memory-based art to visually-based art:**

> Young children's spontaneous copying is not about making perfect imitations or replicas of images of others. It is rather an activity of discovering and developing new systems of graphic equivalences in a child's pictorial language. While it has been suggested that copying lowers children's confidence in self-expressive abilities (Lowenfeld & Brittain, 1987), my studies of young children point to the contrary and indicate that children often see copying as a bridge which allows them to master their visual expression. (Kindler, 1992, pp. 14-15)

Art historians have also questioned the widespread disapproval of copying, arguing that artists frequently copy one another's work and usually produce works that imitate antecedent traditions - two practices that give rise to particular styles or periods.[40] For art historian Annie Smith, "copy wrong" occurs "when no new learning takes place, or worse yet, when wrong information is passed on, or when the same thing is learned over and over" (p. 42).

Developmentalists also believe that commercially-prepared instructional devices, such as colouring books, interfere with the nurturance of self-expression;[41] but even here, long-held assumptions are being challenged. Irvin King (1991) has likened the creative limitations of *colouring* *books* to the recitation of poetry, and their compositional inflexibility to the regulated formats of fugues and sonnets. In a more positive vein, King has further maintained that colouring books facilitate eye-and-hand coordination, provide emotional relief, and reduce performance anxiety.

Romantic-expressive trends

So far we have only discussed scientific-rational trends affecting traditional notions of education through art; however, there are other developing trends that suggest a general movement towards curricular confluency in art education. Specifically, **we can also point to romantic-expressive trends that are affecting traditional notions of education *in* art**:

- cultural pluralism (Bracey, 1990; Chalmers, 1992; Clark, 1992c; Hamblen, 1986; MacGregor, 1979; 1990b).
- feminism (Collins & Sandell, 1984, 1987; Irwin, 1992c; Mansell, 1991; Snider, 1989).
- visual literacy (Lanier, 1982, 1990; Mansell, 1991; Matoba, 1985; Pearse, 1992c).

It is worth noting that these romantic-expressive trends toward cultural pluralism, feminism, and visual literacy all stem from recent developments within the field of critical theory, which Jurgen Habermas (1971) labelled Paradigm III, a *critical-theoretic orientation to forms of knowledge*:

> That paradigm, somewhat underpopulated in 1983, has expanded with increased interest in the social, cultural, and political realities facing art educators and with increased concern for the impact on art education of popular culture, feminism, cultural pluralism, and multiculturalism (Duncum, 1990; Garber, 1990; Mullen & Chalmers, 1990). Indeed, these developments, with their roots firmly in Paradigm III notions of liberation and empowerment of marginalized people, have done much to enrich the texture of contemporary art education. (Pearse, 1992c, p. 247)

Issues of *cultural pluralism* have ranged from the need for pedagogic strategies to accommodate the frequently repressed expressive abilities of children from fundamentalist homes,[42] to the need for "a truly moral art education" which empowers people to distinguish truth from falsehood.[43]

The increasingly *multicultural* composition of contemporary Western society has lead other art educators to investigate:

- whether art curricula should be revised to reduce the cultural shock experienced by immigrant students, and to query to what extent country-of-origin values should be maintained (MacGregor, 1990b).

■ how curricula could be restructured to accommodate both the culturally-universal and the culturally-relative aspects of art (Hamblen, 1986).

■ what racial and religious prejudices have found expression within Western art curricula (Chalmers, 1992).

Feminist perspectives have also enriched traditionally male-oriented and discipline-based approaches to education in art. Georgia Collins and Renee Sandell (1984, 1987) have argued in favour of an "issues approach" to women's "hiddenstream" role in art production, in order to:

■ encourage the interest of female students by providing them with like-sex role models, opportunities for increased pride and self-esteem, and the excitement of discovering a lost heritage;

■ provide all students with a more complete, complex, and provocative picture of artistic activity and achievement in our culture;

■ prepare more realistically those students headed for art careers in which they will find themselves cooperating and competing with artists of both sexes; and

■ stimulate critical thinking with regard to the status and values attached to various art activities in our culture. (1987, p. 13)

Feminist perspectives have grounded articles written by women on other aspects of art education, such as administration (Irwin, 1992c) and teaching (Snider, 1989); but feminist issues have been raised by male educators, as well. Donald Soucy has highlighted the critical role played women in the historical development of the *Nova Scotia College of Art and Design*.[44] In a similar vein, Gidney & Millar have accredited the female accomplishments curricula of the late 1800s for providing a much needed balance within modern secondary schooling.[45]

Recent trends in art education have also focused upon the need for increased attention to *visual literacy* in our schools. The idea that visual form is a type of language that can, and should, be decoded by members of the general public is not new. In the 1970s, Dondis attempted to parallel visual form with written language in terms of grammar and syntax. In the 1980s, Vincent Lanier spoke of visual literacy in terms of aesthetic appreciation. Today, however, visual literacy is frequently linked to either *critical thinking skills*:

Art, or whatever it may be called, becomes one of the three basic skills required to hold, process, and convey school subjects and other significant ideas into a construct that allows children to reason their learning rather than merely represent whatever is presented to them. (Matoba, 1985, p. 46)

or *consumerism*:

Art students need to be provided with the means to critically examine the mass media and its visual language and to be receptive to various forms of cultural production. As producers themselves, their challenge is not to produce novel forms but to produce work which meaningfully and critically interprets the potentially infinite array of cultural forms and interactions. (Pearse, 1992c, pp. 250-251)

Clearly, these developing trends in art education represent new ways of thinking about education through art and education in art. Whether or not they result in a *confluent model of art* from primary to senior grades, only time will tell, but "our future is behind us":

Santayana once said that if we do not know history, we are doomed to repeat it. It is a powerful and useful aphorism. Further, the idea suggests that the seeds of the future are discernable in our history, not as immutable consequence, but as available alternative. In a very real sense, therefore, the future lies behind us; if we look back at our history with care, we will have the opportunity to act so that we bring about a future free of some of the errors of the past. (Lanier, 1990, p.51)

> Art classes then seem to be, in many ways, "model learning environments". I don't want to idealize art teaching, I'm sure as with many subjects, there are good art classes and bad art classes. But the creative impulse and the individual reaction to that impulse is embedded within the structure of art teaching. The classroom is set up, in short, to respond to student initiative and student desire. In this sense, art is the very antithesis of the high status bodies of knowledge which schooling celebrates. (p. 22)
>
> Ivor Goodson (1993)
> Status versus significance in school subject knowledge:
> The Janus face of art education.

Chapter 1 opened with the notion that teaching demands real courage, the courage needed to pursue personal encounters with professional practice. Through such encounters, **teachers bring practice to life, as it were, by animating pedagogy through self.**

The existential nature of educational practice has been increasingly acknowledged by curriculum theorists,[46] and **proponents of self-grounded educational practice are frequently referred to as** *reconceptualists*, a group whose membership includes James Macdonald, Ross Mooney, Paul Klohr, Herbert Kleibard, Philip Phenix, and Maxine Greene:[47]

> Presently, the reconceptualists are focusing on a critique of the field, which they believe is too immersed in practical and technologically oriented approaches to curriculum. They feel that true understanding will come from aesthetic, humanistic, and existential postures. Focusing on understanding oneself will lead to truly heightened consciousness. (Ornstein & Hunkins, 1993, p. 196)

Wilma Longstreet and Harold Shane, in *Curriculum for a New Millennium*, have added *educational existentialism* to Theodore Brameld's (1950) philosophic continuum of *perennialism, essentialism, progressivism*, and *reconstructionism*:

> "Educational existentialism", as we are using the term, places its emphasis on the self as a primary source of

> knowledge about life and its meaning. To achieve
> understanding about life, one must first achieve
> understanding about the self. Whether this is achieved
> subjectively or objectively is a matter for debate both
> philosophically and educationally. The debate, however,
> does not change the essential locus for the derivation of
> knowledge, which is the self. (Longstreet & Shane, 1993, p.
> 118)

Educational existentialism provides an efficacious theoretical base for art
education, in general, and curricula premised upon notions of artistic
disclosure,[48] in particular.

2.1 The need for personal encounters with practice

Teachers as learners

In Longstreet & Shane's description of educational existentialism,
"the essential locus for the derivation of knowledge, which is the self" centred
upon the self as learner. In this chapter, however, **we are going to consider
the notion of educational existentialism from the perspective of the self as
teacher.**

**The importance of the role played by the teacher within educational
practice cannot be overemphasized:**

> We must therefore bear in mind that one of the most
> important factors relating to what children get out of a
> curriculum may be not what is in it, not what use is made
> of it, not how it is taught in terms of techniques of
> instruction, not how the instruction is organised, but who is
> teaching it. ...It follows that any observed difference
> between, for the sake of example, a class taught through
> lectures and a class taught through seminars might have
> nothing at all to do with the manner of instruction, and
> everything to do with the personalities of the individuals
> involved. (Barrow, 1984, p. 27)

**There are two points during the implementation of curriculum when
teachers play especially pivotal roles. The most widely acknowledged point
occurs when teachers are actively involved in instruction, when** *pedagogic
content* **is conveyed to the learner** *(see Figure 4b: Curricular Sequence for Art
Education).* At such times, the notion of a "personal encounter with
professional practice" is most easily understood. Existential concepts such as
the *curricular moment*[49] have been coined to describe these pedagogic
encounters, but the existential focus has usually been upon self as learner:

Yet, in the field of curriculum we confidently talk about "selecting, planning or organizing learning experiences." This confidence begs a question - the question whether we know what it is like when a child "has an experience" or when the child "comes to understand something." (Van Manen, 1990, p. 45)

Existential frameworks have also been developed to describe more extended personal encounters with professional practice. Richard Courtney (1980) speaks of *the dramatic curriculum*; Max van Manen (1991) and Harold Pearse (1992a) talk of *pedagogic thoughtfulness*. But again, the focus remains upon self as learner.

What such self-grounded pedagogies fail to acknowledge is that personal encounters with professional practice need also to be directed toward the teacher's positive being and becoming. **Educational philosophies which place self as the "essential locus for the derivation of knowledge" must function within the context of both learner and teacher. Indeed, the often-heard notion of "teacher as learner" neatly accommodates this dual function and avoids giving the impression that learner and teacher operate as discrete elements within educational practice.**

This might be an appropriate place to mention that while this book speaks primarily of the central role played by student disclosure within art education, we might also talk of the pivotal role played by *teacher disclosure* within professional practice. Many reconceptualists are currently working within this area, and the notion of *the teacher's voice* is a recurring theme in many texts:[50]

Although ethnographic studies and collaborative biographies provide detailed descriptions about the "inside" of a classroom and teacher attitudes, they do not often capture the unique quality of the teacher's voice nor do they conjure up the particular ambience of a crowded classroom. We must encourage the writer, or perhaps I should say, the poets among us - as well as those outside the profession - to engage in the important task of writing eloquent autobiographies and biographies of teachers. (Snider, 1989, p. 48)

Using qualitative methodologies, such as those suggested by Amy Brook Snider, educational existentialists are seeking new insights into self as teacher:

Experiences prior to teaching shape what Pinar calls the architecture of self, which consists of the contribution of the many elements of the private existential person, such as beliefs, values, dispositions, feelings, guiding images, principles whether explicit, implicit, tacit or intuitive. (Butt, Raymond, McCue & Yamagashi, 1992, p. 59)

In this chapter we are concerned with one facet of William Pinar's notion of *the architecture of self*,[51] a facet which focuses upon self as teacher. To identify this element, we need to return to *Figure 4b: Curricular Sequence for Art Education.* We have already discussed the pivotal role played by teachers in the delivery of pedagogic content, but **there is another key point at which teachers engage in personal encounters with professional practice: during the determination of** *pedagogic context.*

Pedagogic context consists of the *curriculum commonplaces* **of learner, milieu, subject, and teacher** (Schwab, 1970).   Curriculum commonplaces form the pedagogic background within most current curricular models, although slight variations are frequently employed. Leslie Huling-Austin and W. Robert Houston, for example, speak of *antecedent variables* which they define as "conditions and variables that affect teacher education, that, while not directly related to process, influence, guide, and even direct that process".[52] Huling-Austin and Houston offer four antecedent variables: learner characteristics, teacher characteristics, environmental culture, and instructional conditions.   Clearly, these antecedent variables correspond closely to our own Schwabian pedagogic context, with the notable exception of the last element, instructional conditions, which are discussed in terms of "videotape players, computers, instructional supplies, and materials".[53]

Curiously missing from the Huling-Austin and Houston model is Schwab's *subject* commonplace.   **Models of curriculum which ignore discipline-based factors and treat school subjects as interchangeable curricular clones often foster considerable opposition from practitioners.**[54] To emphasize the importance of this point, one so fundamental to the concept of pedagogic subcultures, we shall investigate in some detail the process of curricular reform undertaken by the Ontario Ministry of Education during the 1980s.

School subjects and curricular reform

Pressures for curricular reform in Ontario came from three constituencies: students, parents, and universities. Perhaps the most unusual of these involved a lack of students, since the end of the baby boom had resulted in severe declines in secondary school enrollments. Fewer students in Ontario high schools meant several things to the profession, such as the dismissal of junior teachers, the shrinkage of provincial grants to school boards, and a general downsizing of school operations.

The decade also faced demands from parents for more structured secondary school curricula. The student-centred ideals of the 1967 provincial report *Living and Learning*[55] had never taken firm root, in either Ontario classrooms or living rooms. The back-to-the-basics bandwagon had begun to roll.

The third force actively promoting school reform was propelled by various Ontario universities. Admission officers suggested that several secondary school graduation courses offered insufficient academic preparation for university study. The discontinuation of provincial high school graduation examinations, the development of curricula by boards of education, and the relatively small number of compulsory school credits all contributed to a demand by universities for increased provincial control over secondary education, not for higher quality but for greater consistency.

This trio of reform agents brought on a flurry of provincial studies including the *Secondary Education Review Project* (SERP) in 1980, the *Report on the Secondary Education Review Project* (ROSE) in 1981, and the *Commission on Declining Enrollments* (CODE). In 1984 the Ontario Ministry of Education mandated new regulations within *Ontario Schools: Intermediate and Senior Divisions* (OS:IS).

The breadth and depth of educational reforms prescribed by *OS:IS* made the revision of all provincial subject guidelines an urgent necessity. One of the very first guidelines issued under *OS:IS* was *Visual Arts: Intermediate and Senior Divisions*,[56] a document that continues to provoke opposition from many Ontario art educators.[57]

A critical analysis of *OS:IS* reveals its fundamental rejection of pedagogic variances among secondary school subjects. **Through the dual channels of regulation and prescription, *OS:IS* treated subjects as largely indistinguishable curricular blocks. For all school subjects, *OS:IS* imposed a trio of pedagogic commonalities: (a) a prescribed set of educational goals; (b) a regulated framework for courses of study; and (c) a disposition towards academic disciplines.**

OS:IS began by issuing 13 *educational goals*, which mandated student growth in areas as diverse as "environmental respect" and "the common welfare of society." An early draft of *Visual Arts* gave clear evidence of the degree to which subject guidelines were crafted from these generic educational goals. In response to *OS:IS* goal #4, "(to) develop physical fitness and good health," members of the draft document writing team suggested that teachers lead art students in calisthenic exercises at their desks prior to studio activities. Goal #7, "(to) develop an understanding of the role of the individual within the family and the role of the family within society," generated the objective that art teachers "ensure their students develop an adequate level of heterosexual growth." These goals were removed from the final version as a result of criticisms from practitioners during the draft document's field validation, but *Visual Arts* (along with every subsequent *OS:IS*-based subject guideline) maintained that all 13 *OS:IS* educational goals were germane to the study of art in Ontario.

Prior to *OS:IS*, Ontario had offered 9 *levels of difficulty* upon which local curricular documents could be developed. One of these, level 9, was termed open or non-streamed; it was widely used in small enrollment areas, such as art. *OS:IS*, however, narrowed these down to 3: advanced, general, and basic. Schools were expected to offer courses in all subjects based upon at least two of these levels of difficulty. Such regulations made sense for compulsory subjects, such as English, where the student population produced high course registrations across all three levels. Such regulations, however, didn't make sense for optional subjects, such as art. The educational reform strategies implemented by the Ministry, however, did not recognize such subject-based variances. The imposition of a common framework for courses of study forced many art departments to cancel courses, accept bi-level/bi-grade classes, or abandon advanced level courses entirely (which precluded student entry to university art courses).

The third strategic commonality underpinning Ontario's reform of secondary school education was a disposition towards academic disciplines. *OS:IS* instituted a common graduation diploma based upon the completion of 30 courses (16 compulsory/14 optional). Pre-*OS:IS* students were streamed into four- and five-year programmes (Ontario formerly offered grade 13) and received, accordingly, different graduation credentials. Ironically, this "upgrading" of graduation requirements resulted in fewer graduation course requirements for university-bound students.

The *OS:IS* disposition towards academic disciplines could be clearly seen within its 16 compulsory courses. The 16 specified courses were overwhelmingly academic; for example, students were required to complete only 1 course in business or technological studies. The limited number of optional courses, 14 of 30, reduced the ability of students to select a range of optional subjects, and retained the emphasis upon academic courses. A parallel system of pre-requisites further penalized optional subjects. Subjects selected in grades 9 and 10 were critical; the pre-requisite system made it very difficult for students to change subject areas or levels of difficulty during their senior years. General- or basic-level students could not easily join the ranks of the academically advanced.

The disposition towards academic disciplines was exemplified in the creation by *OS:IS* of *Ontario Academic Courses* (OACs). These were designed to replace grade 13 in Ontario and to respond to the universities' demand for consistent levels of academic preparedness among secondary school graduates. Given the main goal of greater student preparation for university study, the academic nature of OACs came as no surprise. The visual arts OAC was typical: 50% of the course was devoted to the study of 120 master artworks prescribed in the 1986 *Visual Arts* guideline; the remaining 50% was for studio. The studio portion presented the creative process as an academic, visual essay. Students were to begin by identifying a problem that they wished to resolve through drawing, supported by only **one** of: painting, printmaking, sculpture, or photography. The artifacts produced were only worth 30%; 20% was assigned to a written proposal and an accumulated information file. The art history portion of the OAC was completely academic: 10% for a written paper, 20% for a final examination, and 20% for various tests. Clearly, the visual arts OAC accepted the *OS:IS* disposition towards academic disciplines: 70% of the course was devoted to *knowledge about art*, only 30% for *knowledge in art*.

Data garnered during the *OAC Visual Arts Examination Review*[58] suggested widespread teacher resistance to the visual arts guideline. The *Review* was conducted by the Ministry using a format devised earlier for review of the English OAC, another example of its disregard for discipline-sensitive implementation strategies. *Review* highlights included: (a) 29% of secondary schools declined to participate in the study; (b) 62% non-conformity to requirements for written examinations; and (c) 60% non-conformity to requirements for portfolio evaluations. These three pieces of data provided insight into the rate of adoption by art teachers of the reforms mandated by *OS:IS*. Obviously, the visual arts guideline had met with considerable teacher apathy and outright opposition.

The *OAC Visual Arts Examination Review* demonstrated that the implementation of curricular reforms can be effectively resisted by classroom practitioners. Lately, many sociological elements of educational reform, of which teacher resistance to change is but one example, have been the foci of Canadian educational research. Roger Clark (1991a) has used a sociologically-based model of curricular development[59] to investigate art as an emergent school subject. Ivor Goodson (1987, 1988, 1992) and Ardra Cole (1991) have explored how teachers' life histories affect curricula. Richard Courtney (1980, 1982, 1989) has outlined how the social dynamics of play may be utilized to promote effective learning throughout school curricula.

Recently, the notion of *antecedent subject subcultures* has been developed by researchers working within The Research Unit on Classroom Learning and Computer Use in Schools (RUCCUS), housed at the Faculty of Education, The University of Western Ontario:

> To some extent each subject in the secondary school is a separate microcosm, a microworld with varying values and traditions. In a real sense we found evidence that teachers experience their subjects as separate "subcultures".... [There is a] perceived need for some subjects to be taught in different ways from others, in order to allow for the distinctive character of the subject to be transmitted more effectively. (Goodson, Mangan & Rhea, 1991, p. 4)

Goodson's previous studies provided a complementary research strand to the exploration of antecedent subject subcultures, namely, *teachers' life histories*:

> More than one teacher in this project has said that teaching style is an expression of a teacher's personality. If this is true, the implication is that a change in style would require

nothing less than a change in personality. The difficulty of enforcing such a change should be obvious. ...

In the life-history interviews, teachers have often expressed two basic themes regarding their teaching philosophies. First, that they care deeply about their students, and are interested in opening up some form of novel learning experiences for them. Second, that their teaching styles derive directly from their concept of education and its intersection with their personal lifestyles. (Goodson, Mangan & Rhea, 1991, p. 7)

The RUCCUS researchers investigated the implementation of *computer-aided learning* (CAL) at two secondary schools over a three year period. Their findings stressed that **levels of teacher resistance to, or acceptance of, curricular change were closely linked to both antecedent subject subcultures and teachers' life histories**. Neither of these two concepts were incorporated into Ontario's approach to curricular reform during the 1980s. The inference to be made is not that these allied concepts ensure the successful implementation of curricular change by themselves; on the contrary, the complexity of educational theory suggests that successful implementation requires an inclusive approach, one which tackles change from a variety of angles.

2.2   The reality of pedagogic subcultures

This book is premised upon the belief that antecedent subject subcultures and teachers' life histories play important roles in overall professional practice, as well as in the process of curricular reform. **Viewed jointly, antecedent subject subcultures and teachers' life histories produce the phenomena of *pedagogic subcultures*, a reality that lies at the very heart of "personal encounters with professional practice"**.

It is important to understand that pedagogic subcultures involve both subject and teacher commonplaces. Thus, the concept of pedagogic subcultures goes beyond the scope of *pedagogic content knowledge*,[60] which is rooted primarily in content expertise alone:

Just as an artist's representation of his or her artistic vision is shaped by a combination of artistic abilities, ideas, media, and so forth, the teaching of artistic concepts to students is shaped by the teacher's understandings and interpretations of art content, art teaching, and general classroom procedures. Art teachers merge and use both their knowledge of content and pedagogy to present subject matter to students in specific classroom settings. (Bullock & Galbraith, 1992, p. 87)

Constructing a pedagogic profile for art

If acknowledgement of and respect for pedagogic subcultures are necessary conditions for personal encounters with practice, we should be able to construct a profile of characteristics, or attributes, for individual subcultures. Certainly, we cannot construct a definitive profile of art as a pedagogic subculture; a range of profiles would be needed to address geographic and social idiosyncrasies specific to given educational populations. Several recent Canadian studies, however, offer glimpses into a Canadian profile for art. It should be noted that the research context of each study will be presented in the briefest of formats, and that highlights will be restricted to only those findings relevant to the construction of our profile.

> **Study 1**
>
> A cross-Canada study of high school art teachers.
> (Gray & MacGregor, 1990a, 1990b, 1991)

James Gray and Ronald MacGregor's research focused upon three questions: what factors in art teachers' personal experience and interests affect the organization and conduct of their classes; what kinds of classroom interactions characterize the conduct of art programs; and how are art teacher priorities and attitudes embodied in classroom environments and art products?

The researchers undertook a series of observational case studies between 1985 and 1988, visiting 59 secondary schools across Canada. The collected data were analyzed within three content headings: teacher background and perceived professional role; conduct of classroom activities; and space, equipment, and products.

The study suggested that a pedagogic subculture profile for art would be highly irregular, diversified, and extensively coloured by individual practitioners. Further, the data suggested that the adoption by art teachers of prescriptive curricula, such as Ontario's guideline for visual arts, would not be facilitated by the idiosyncratic nature of art education. Thus, Gray & MacGregor's study helps to explain the high rates of teacher resistance to the guideline as reported in the 1989 Ontario *OAC Visual Arts Examination Review*.

Gray & MacGregor stressed, however, that the lack of uniformity within art did not mean that a profile could not be constructed:

Yet, idiosyncrasy is not synonymous with whimsy. Individual temperament affected the selection of experiences that the teacher considered to be in the students' best interests, and determined whether the space in which art education was conducted was treated as a workshop or a shrine. Each teacher surveyed would, however, have admitted that the other informants were teaching a form of art. Although they enjoy an autonomy partly attributable to art's non-examination status in provincial systems, and partly to the Western tradition of individuals that surrounds the arts, teachers have evidently fashioned their programs from a common body of material. (p. 56)

Thus, we can begin the construction of a profile for art as a unique, pedagogic subculture by recognizing the crucial role that individual temperament plays in the selection of art activities and the environment in which those activities take place. High levels of autonomy, within individual teachers and art itself, are also key elements in the profile. Finally, the study suggests that high levels of eclecticism and acceptance of diversity characterize the teaching of art at the secondary school level in Canada.

Study 2

A case study of microcomputers in art education.
Qualitative educational research studies:
Methodologies in transition.
Blomeyer (1991)

Robert Blomeyer's ethnographically-oriented descriptive study tracked the implementation of computer-aided learning (CAL) within two settings: a comprehensive high school with studio-based art classes taught in a traditional manner, and a vocational high school having a highly-specialized graphics program. The former had three distributively-networked microcomputers and a colour printer; the latter was configured with a central laboratory with 20 networked workstations and two colour printers. **A shared pedagogic subculture within both art settings was observed by Blomeyer who stressed the individualized, circular, and distributive attributes of art pedagogy throughout his report:**

In both settings, student activity was highly individualized and both art teachers supported this individual activity by distributing their support activity throughout the group of students under their supervision. (p. 212)

One outstanding similarity is obvious in the two observed situations. The art teachers in both cases displayed similar circulating behaviour while they were monitoring student studio work. They typically moved quickly and smoothly around the studio or microcomputer lab setting, answered questions, offered assistance when requested, commented supportively about the students' efforts, and only occasionally redirected students' efforts if the observed activity of a particular individual went outside the established boundaries for proper technique and conduct. (p. 213)

Certainly, this trio of pedagogic attributes are not unique to art classes, as they can be observed in most any other subject area; however, do they appear with sufficiently greater frequency in art classes that they can sustain the notion of a pedagogic subculture for art? Support for an affirmative response to this question was found in the following study.

Study 3

Closing the circle: Conclusions and recommendations.
Curriculum and context in the use of computers for classroom learning: Summative report, Volume 3
(Goodson, Mangan & Rhea, 1991)

This three-year RUCCUS study into the implementation of CAL at the secondary school level involved the following subject areas: art, family studies, social studies, and technological studies. Previous references from this study have suggested the existence of pedagogic subcultures within the two research schools.

The RUCCUS research officers developed a system for tabulating observed classroom activity on two basic dimensions: interpersonal interactions and levels of cognitive function. This became known as the *RUCCUS Interaction Analysis/Cognitive Patterns Tracking System* (RIACPTS). RIACPTS data allowed the quantitative analyses of pedagogic phenomena among teachers and across subjects.

Two statistically significant pedagogic phenomena separated the art teachers, and art as a subject, from the other groups. First, **the art teachers spent significantly (.05 level) less time devoted to teacher questioning and pupil response activities than did teachers in the other subject areas.** Such activities accounted for a mean proportion of almost 20% of social studies class time but less than 5% of art classes. As well, **the art teachers spent**

significantly more time devoted to small group teaching activities than did teachers in the other subject areas. An average of 90% of art time was devoted to such activities whereas social studies spent less than 50%.

Study 4

Principal investigator's report: Art.
Curriculum and context in the use of computers for classroom learning: Summative report, Volume 2.
(Clark, 1991d)

In this RUCCUS report I summarized the data collected from the art segment of Study 3. I analyzed the computer-based art activities using a functional *typology of learner/CAL interactions* developed by UNCAL (Kemmis, Atkin, & Wright, 1977). No examples of art-based CAL curricula were noted within the three lowest levels of interaction tasks: *recognition* (yes-or-no responses), *recall* (fill-in-the-blank responses), or *reconstructive understanding* (multiple choice responses). *Global reconstructive* tasks were often observed. Student responses in this category were open-ended; their assessment involved not only the correct application of program content but extension requiring analytic, synthetic, and creative solutions. *Constructive understanding* tasks were also common. Original knowledge or constructions were required; they were assessed relative to their application to relevant functional frameworks.

I also analyzed the computer-based art activities within a *taxonomic model of cognitive activities* developed by MacDonald, Atkin, Jenkins, & Kemmis (1977). *Instructional CAL*, involving drill, practice, and tutorial activities, were limited to brief, teacher-lead demonstrations. *Revelatory CAL*, utilizing simulations and trial-and-error exercises, were frequently observed within the context of play opportunities directly after instructional CAL episodes. Students and teachers often compared typical revelatory activities to the production of rough work in more traditional studio processes. Play was identified as an attribute of the art profile in all of the cited studies[61] making it one of the premier attributes of the pedagogic subculture. *Conjectural CAL*, relating to the creation of new knowledge, was the most frequently observed cognitive activity, a predictable result for a subject centred so heavily upon student creativity. *Emancipatory CAL*, encompassing activities that free individuals from routine, time-consuming tasks, prompted a mixed response. Computers were often used by the art teachers in the preparation of teaching materials but rarely for the compilation of student grades.

The cited Canadian studies suggest several attributes with which the construction of a skeletal characteristic profile for art as a pedagogic subculture can be initiated.   Clearly, much more research needs to be undertaken before a Canadian profile can be sketched with confidence.   It is anticipated that profiles for art pedagogic subcultures will vary among countries and between regions due to variant geographic and social conditions; future comparisons should prove quite interesting.

The data from the four Canadian art studies indicate that art classes require a different emphasis in the kinds of student activities and in the role of the teacher, than do subjects such as geography or family studies. The four studies suggest that generic attributes for art profiles should include:

> **pedagogic eclecticism; acceptance of diversity; individualized, circular, and distributive instructional patterns; small group teaching activities; play-based learning episodes; and high-order cognition.** (Clark, 1992d, p. 112)

The construction of profiles for other school subjects will be required before the utility of pedagogic subcultures can be tested during future attempts at curricular reform.   Once an array of profiles is available, curriculum specialists should be able to implement change with a much greater degree of sensitivity to the needs of practitioners across the educational spectrum.

We have devoted much time to the proposition that school reforms which ignore pedagogic subcultures are likely to be either benignly ignored or actively opposed by practitioners.   It bears repeating, however, that successful educational reforms need to be sensitive to all four curriculum commonplaces.   For example, Hodgkinson (1991) has focused upon learner and milieu commonplaces, which collectively make up *community subcultures (see Figure 4b: Curricular Sequence for Art Education)*:

> Basically, the publication of *A Nation at Risk* marked the return of the owners after a long absence to find education's house badly deteriorated. ...Since that time, a blizzard of education reform proposals has fallen, and states have raised the graduation standards for high schools, installed minimum standards for moving from one grade to the next, required new teachers to pass special examinations before being allowed to teach, instituted choice and magnet school programs and so on.
>
> But so far, there has been no change in high school graduation rates, in most test scores, or in other indicators of "quality."   After nearly a decade, we have fixed the plaster in education's house, installed new windows, and

repaired the electric motors. *But the roof still leaks.* Until we fix the roof, the house continues to deteriorate. (p. 10)

Harold Hodgkinson uses the leaky roof as a metaphor for the 33% of students in the United States whose impoverished backgrounds place them "at risk of school failure even before they enter kindergarten" (p. 10). He argues that school reforms must focus upon improved levels of *school preparedness*, especially within low-income and minority learner populations. Although his call for massive increases in levels of school preparedness is obviously commendable, leaks in roofs cannot be stopped through the acquisition of new and improved occupants. The leaky roof will continue to let in rain until the work crew is sufficiently persuaded to begin the needed repairs. In other words, past educational reforms have been unsuccessful because teachers have not been sufficiently persuaded to implement them.[62]

Status versus significance

We do not need to focus on the macro-level of educational reform in order to see the need for curricula that address the unique attributes of pedagogic subcultures. A quick visit to any school staff lounge will demonstrate how pedagogic subcultures affect the micro-level of daily professional practice. **Art teachers are notorious for being "different". Their views on professional practice, both within and beyond their studios, are very frequently at odds with the general school environment.**

This chapter began with a quote from an article entitled, "Status versus significance in school subject knowledge: The Janus face of art education". In that 1993 paper, Ivor Goodson discussed the case study of a young art teacher conducted in the United Kingdom by Peter Woods (1984). Woods' study sought to discover "to what extent does this teacher find self expression within the curriculum, [and] how far is a subject "as practised" in the classroom a realization of an individual teacher's self?" (p. 239).

Goodson's summary of the study will probably come as a surprise to few practitioners. **Wood's art teacher felt that the school's overall curriculum was decontextualised and not capable of nurturing creative, well-disposed young adults.** To survive in such an environment, the art teacher focused upon his classroom, his own "little island".

The *marginality of art education* springs from its efforts to encourage learning in all students:

The state system of schooling has always over privileged the minority that will go on to university education and has tended to pervert the whole system of public schooling towards the provision of those bodies of knowledge which will service the professionalised minority. The majority of our school populations has traditionally been thrown to the wolves.

> Hence subjects which have made their concern the
> creativity and teaching of all children, art is one example,
> technological studies would be another, environmental
> studies was the one I gave earlier and so on, tend to have
> their status and resources reduced because they are not
> exclusively concerned with the preparation of a professional
> minority through university education. (Goodson, 1993, p.
> 24)

As is frequently the case, there is a positive side to this dilemma.
**The factors that work to marginalize art education, and subsequently reduce
its *status* within the educational milieu, are the same elements that lend
significance to art education:**

> Perhaps then, in some ways, art for all the problems of
> status and resources that it faces is in a very fortunate
> position in terms of the educational possibilities it provides
> for its students - and I can think of no better criteria for
> definition of a school subject. ...For many children then and
> for the teachers within them, art classrooms, even given the
> problems of status, remain deeply significant centres of
> creativity and educational exploration. Long may it be so.
> (p. 24).

2.3   The search for unity, integration, and identity

**In Section 1.1 our investigation into the divergent roots of art
education chronicled a tale of curricular competition: internal competition
among proponents of art as methodology or art as discipline, and external
competition between art and other school subjects.** But the emergence of
art education was not unique. Dance, drama, and music education
encountered similar competing forces, and **within most school-based
curricula arts education emerged as two solitudes: education *through* art(s)
at the elementary level, and education *in* art(s) at the secondary level.**

Arts educators can, perhaps, take solace in the recognition that these
two solitudes reflect "streams of influence" within the wider field of
education:

> Throughout the century art education was strongly
> influenced by developments affecting general education.
> Fads, fashions, movements, and causes came and went,
> arising in two main streams of influence, one that
> harboured a scientific rational tendency while the other,
> labelled as a romantic-expressionist tendency, preferred
> freer modes of thinking and action. (Efland, 1990b, p. 133)

The disunity within art education can also be rationalized through references to the historical separation of elementary and secondary schooling,[63] and the pressures exerted periodically by university scholars in the determination of secondary school curricula.[64]

Bridging elementary and secondary curricula

While such perspectives may offer solace, they must not be allowed to foster complacency, for students need to experience art as a *curricular continuum*, not as polarized solitudes:

> The primary challenge to art education during the 1990s may well be the resolution of these conflicting philosophies. The curricular battle ground will surely be the junior/intermediate division, currently neutral territory populated by unsuspecting generalists. Any successful curricular bridge will require the concerted efforts of practitioners, scholars, and administrators. (Clark, 1992b, p. 26)

Within the field of general education, the central issue of how best to bridge elementary and secondary education has never been satisfactorily resolved. Many school boards continue to maintain separate elementary and secondary schools, while others operate senior elementary or junior high schools. Some boards of education have developed the concept of middle schools, avoiding any references to elementary or secondary education altogether.

Attempts to cross this great divide have usually involved politically-motivated crusades designed to extend elementary practices into upper grades or secondary practices into lower grades. For example, in 1984 the Ontario Ministry of Education included grades 7 and 8 in its regulatory document for secondary schools *Ontario Schools: Intermediate and Senior Divisions* (OS:IS), only to contradict itself in 1993 by issuing *The Common Curriculum, Grades 1-9*, a regulatory document for elementary schools which included grade 9. Neither document was premised upon a coherent K-12 learning continuum; the former was a purely *subject-based secondary model*, and the latter a wholly *outcomes-based elementary model*.

It is important to note that such attempts have rarely sought to achieve a K-12 dominance; rather, they have undertaken a form of trench warfare that measured success in terms of the acquisition of one or two additional grades. The reason for this stalemate at the curricular front is not hard to understand. Any full assault aimed at complete victory would result in eventual defeat. The prospect of grade 1 students attending a school organized on a secondary model would simply go beyond the pale of reason: just try to imagine six-year-old Johnny on a completely rotarized timetable, cramming for examinations, and failing his final in mathematics. Similarly, the prospect of grade 12 students attending a school organized on a typical elementary model would also be unacceptable to the general public.

A K-12 continuum can only be achieved when elementary and secondary models are seen as valid segments of the whole, rather than as viable pathways for the entire length of the continuum. Elementary curricula based upon models of child development and cognition work because they build upon pedagogic realities that exist at the elementary level. But learners grow up and subject matter increases in complexity. As pedagogic realities evolve, so must pedagogic responses. By themselves, neither elementary nor secondary models can provide a viable pathway for a complete K-12 continuum, for each represents a unique pedagogic response to a different segment of professional practice.

Efforts have been made to provide internal unity to art curricula, as well; unfortunately, they have fallen prey to the same misguided strategies used to unify elementary and secondary models within general education. For example, proponents of art as methodology have sought to extend their child-centred notions of cognitive development, such as play,[65] into secondary grades. *The dramatic curriculum* (Courtney, 1980) and *education through art* (Read, 1943) are elementary models that purport to be applicable from K-12. The language used in such paradigms, however, provides early evidence of their ultimate inability to provide effective continua K-12. Both the dramatic curriculum and education through art speak eloquently to the developmental needs of young children, and both address these needs through pedagogic responses that reflect the pedagogic realities of elementary schooling. But just as early educators erred in viewing children as "miniature adults",[66] many contemporary proponents of art as methodology falter by failing to recognize that teenagers are not "bigger children." Herbert Read's central goal "to retain the innocent eye, the instinctive sensibility of childhood"[67] is not capable of providing a K-12 continuum for art education, for it fails to acknowledge that, with the possible exception of Peter Pan, little boys and girls do (and should) grow up.

Similarly, proponents of art as discipline have also tried to provide internal unity to art education by extending their secondary school models of art education into lower grades. One of the most recent, and one of the most vigorous, attempts has been undertaken by the *Getty Center for Education in the Arts* through its promotion of *discipline-based art education* (DBAE). DBAE is a typical secondary model, especially in terms of its conception by university-based scholars. The roots of DBAE can be traced to an influential group of university scholars in the 1960s:

> In 1965 a Seminar in Art Education Research and Curriculum Development was held at Pennsylvania State University (Mattil, 1966). The pervasive theme presented by such noted scholars as Barkan, Broudy, Eisner and Chapman, centred upon the idea that art or art education

is a discipline in its own right. A predominant concern raised at the conference focused upon the task of making the structure of art clear enough so that curriculum planners could build a structure of sequential concepts for organized learning. Art knowledge had to be perceived therefore from the expert point of view, that is, from the characteristic processes artists, historians, and critics use in their work. In turn, these "models" could be emulated by students as they proceeded through inquiries in art. (Irwin, 1991b, p. 35)

The notion that young art students could, or should, emulate "characteristic processes artists, historians, and critics use in their work" parallels the misguided notion that teenagers should learn within the same play-centred parameters that children use. While the university-oriented model of DBAE might very well be capable of being adapted to the pedagogic realities of secondary school art education, its emphases upon studio, art history, art criticism, and aesthetics become increasingly untenable within junior and primary grades. Children do not have the ability to identify, let alone assess, abstract aesthetic concepts, nor do they have the ability to comprehend, let alone empathize, with the cultural aspirations of civilizations long past. In summary, discipline-based models are likely incapable of providing unity within art curricula K-12 because they respond poorly to the pedagogic realities of elementary schooling.

This is not to suggest that curricular models based upon *art as methodology* or *art as discipline* are categorically incapable of being used as K-12 curricular continua. Students throughout history have been subjected to all kinds of educational models; the *learner commonplace*[68] is remarkably flexible. The point being made, however, is that **elementary and secondary pedagogic strategies work best on their home turf; their efficacy declines steadily as their ability to respond pedagogically to changes in the learner commonplace declines**.

Ultimately, **internal unity within art curricula K-12 will only be achieved through the consensual adoption of a pedagogic commonality that respects and responds to the intrinsic values of existing elementary and secondary art curricula**. Such a commonality will need to reflect aspects of both process and product, as well as the essences of both education through art and education in art. This book identifies *artistic disclosure* as just such a pedagogic commonality, a proposition which is discussed at length within *Chapter 3: Art in Theory*.

Internal competition among the arts

Our study into the emergence of art education in Chapter 1 also highlighted the degree to which curricular competition has pitted the arts internally against each other, and externally against the wider array of school subjects.

Internal competition amongst the arts has paradoxically been heightened in recent years by increased public acceptance of the value of arts education. Whereas during most of this century elementary schools had only to accommodate art and music, many jurisdictions have recently mandated drama and dance education, as well. Given the crowded curriculum that exists within current elementary schooling, time for these additional arts subjects has been difficult to appropriate.

Within primary grades, the prevalence of arts as methodology as the dominant pedagogic vehicle for the delivery of art, dance, drama, and music education has largely solved this dilemma. The gradual emergence of the arts as distinct subjects within senior elementary grades, however, has required more discipline-based curricular solutions.

Perhaps the most common suggestion put forth, and usually the one favoured by educational administrators, has been that the four arts subjects be delivered using an integrated approach. The integrated approach fits easily within the interdisciplinary foundation of elementary schooling and can be supported through references to the *arts-in-education movement* of the 1970s, whose "first characteristic was its emphasis upon arts in the plural".[69] Integrated models are frequented cited as practical solutions to the crowded curriculum in contemporary education:

> An integrated curriculum also has the potential to alleviate the problems of curriculum overload and fragmentation. As society changes and the frontiers of knowledge expand, the curriculum is under pressure to accommodate new material. A curriculum organized along traditional lines becomes a constantly expanding body of knowledge that must somehow be fitted into a finite school day. By contrast, a curriculum that focuses on the relationships between subjects promotes learning that applies to several disciplines at the same time, and may allow teachers to streamline curriculum. (Ontario Ministry of Education and Training, 1993b, p. 2)

At first glance, the adoption of integrated arts curricula within intermediate grades seems the obvious way to proceed, and for many school jurisdictions it may well be the best solution. It would seem prudent at this point, however, to address the issue of integration more fully, for as is the case so often with "obvious" answers, integration is a far more complex issue than it appears to be.

Models of curricular integration

First, it should be made clear that the issue of curricular integration is not new; effective teachers, yes, even subject specialists, have always planned integrative activities for their students. **Nor is the primary issue whether or not subject areas themselves should be integrated for organizational purposes; rather, it is a question of how best to integrate** *subject matter.*

Second, the issue of integration should not sidetracked by ancillary issues, such as the availability of practitioners capable of implementing integrated curricula at the secondary school level; nor should the merits of integration be coloured by political realities, such as the known tendency of administrators to support integrated arts as a means of covering four subject areas within the same time span formerly allotted to just art and music education.

Third, any discussion related to the merits of integration needs to be preceded by an explicit explanation of just what is meant by integration, for there are several accepted models from which to choose. Indeed, it may come as a deep shock to some advocates of integration to learn that **traditional subject-based curricula represent a perfectly valid form of integration**: "Individual subjects continue to be useful ways of organizing learning, since we need to present concepts and skills to students in a systematic way." (Ontario Ministry of Education and Training, 1993b, p. 2)

Robin Fogarty has outlined ten approaches to integration, which can be grouped within three broad categories:

> Beginning with an exploration *within single disciplines* (the fragmented, connected, and nested models), and continuing with models that integrate *across several disciplines* (the sequenced, shared, webbed, threaded, and integrated models), the continuum ends with models that operate *within* learners themselves (the immersed model) and finally *across* networks of learners (the networked model). (Fogarty, 1991b, p. 61)

Fogarty's ten approaches are described within *Figure 2a: Models of Integration.*

Clearly, the concept of integration really is very complex. It is not simply "an attack on the subject-structured curriculum";[70] fully 8 of Fogarty's ten models presuppose the continued existence of subject disciplines within school curricula. **The notion that integration operates in direct opposition to subject disciplines stems from a mistaken belief that** *integration* **is synonymous with** *interdisciplinary*:

> The very notion of integration incorporates the idea of unity between forms of knowledge and their respective disciplines. Interdisciplinary on the other hand simply refers to the use of more than one discipline in pursuing a particular inquiry. (Pring, 1973, p. 135)

The durability of subject areas has often been ascribed to the self-serving actions of subject specialists within secondary schools:

Within Single Disciplines

Fragmented	The traditional model of separate and distinct disciplines, which fragments the subject areas.
Connected	Within each subject area, course content is connected topic to topic, concept to concept, one year's work to the next, and related idea(s) explicitly.
Nested	Within each subject area, the teacher targets multiple skills: a social, a thinking skill, and a content-specific skill.

Across Several Disciplines

Sequenced	Topics or units of study are rearranged and sequenced to coincide with one another. Similar ideas are taught in concert while remaining separate subjects.
Shared	Shared planning and teaching take place in two disciplines in which overlapping concepts or ideas emerge as organizing elements.
Webbed	A fertile theme is webbed to curriculum contents and disciplines; subjects use the theme to sift out appropriate concepts, topics, and ideas.
Threaded	The metacurricular approach threads thinking skills, social skills, multiple intelligences, technology and study skills through the various disciplines.
Integrated	This interdisciplinary approach matches subjects for overlaps in topics and concepts with some team teaching in an authentic integrated model.

Within and Across Learners

Immersed	The disciplines become part of the learner's lens of expertise; the learner filters all content through this lens and becomes immersed in his or her own experience.
Networked	The learner filters all learning through the expert's eye and makes internal connections that lead to external networks of experts in related fields.

Figure 2a: Models of Integration

(Fogarty, 1991a, 1991b)

> Subjects have tended to become preserves belonging to specialist teachers; barriers have been erected between them, and teachers have felt unqualified or not free to trespass upon the dominions of other teachers. The specific values of each subject have been pressed to the neglect of the values common to several or all. The school course has come to resemble the "hundred yards" course, each subject following a track marked off from the others by a tape. In the meantime we feel, the child is apt to be forgotten. (Goodson, 1987, p. 31)

Does this sound familiar? Actually, in this passage curriculum theorist Ivor Goodson has quoted from the *Norwood Report*, written for the British government in 1943. Obviously, the debate over how schools should be organized is neither new nor resolved.

A less cynical explanation for the durability of school subjects has been put forward by Philip Phenix, who suggests that **reliance upon subject areas improves the quality of instruction**:

> One of the secrets of good teaching is the practice of clearly charting a way through the subject of instruction so that the students know how each topic as it comes along fits into the whole scheme of the course and of the discipline to which it belongs. They understand where they are in relation to what has gone before and to what is to be studied subsequently. The effect of such teaching is a growing appreciation of the inner logic of the subject, resulting at length in a grasp of its spirit and method which will be proof against the erosions of detailed forgetting. (Phenix, 1960, p. 307)

Similarly, **repeated calls for the replacement of subjects by thematic units have encountered criticism, too**:

> We have recently heard of proposals to integrate courses around the themes of "Canada" and "sidewalks" (because they lead everywhere). The mere joining together of various elements under the rubric of a common theme does not integrate the study in any educationally productive way. Ironically, organizing curriculum around loosely defined themes may increase the amount of curricular fragmentation. (Case, 1992, p. 35)

The pros and cons of organizing curricula by school subjects are inextricably linked to parallel debates concerning the merits of *generalist versus specialist* orientations within education.[71] Given such perspectives, it is not difficult to understand why the issue of subject areas has proven to be a lightning rod for curricular debates among elementary and secondary teachers. Nonetheless, the idea that knowledge is not a singular entity, but a grouping of disparate *types of knowledge*, has been around since Aristotle organized knowledge into *theoretical* (science and mathematics), *practical* (politics and ethics), and *productive* (music and architecture).[72] We can find similar ideas expressed today within Howard Gardner's *theory of multiple intelligences*, which suggests seven types of knowledge.[73]

Thus, while schooling has always been organized upon "types of knowledge", curricula do not need to be organized upon subject areas per se. **One method frequently put forward as a practical way of reducing the territorial rigidity of school subjects is the clustering of similar disciplines.** For example, the Ontario Ministry of Education and Training's 1993 regulatory document *The Common Curriculum, Grades 1-9* clusters curricula around four "core areas": language; the arts; self and society; mathematics, science, and technology. The method of implementation is not mandated; Robin Fogarty's ten models of integration are suggested as possible alternatives. It is worth mentioning, however, that *The Common Curriculum, Grades 1-9* rarely manages to stop referring to traditional subject disciplines, despite its stated assumption that "to demonstrate the connections between ideas, people, and phenomena, those developing curriculum should focus on broad program areas rather than narrowly defined subjects and disciplines" (p. 13).

Clustering the arts

Many school systems which have elected to cluster curricula employ the concept of the *collective arts*, which in provinces such as Saskatchewan and Ontario involves art, dance, drama, and music education. The proposal that the four arts subjects could, or should, be clustered is not without controversy. Proponents often cite claims put forth by the *arts-in-education* movement of the 1960s and 1970s, a movement characterized by:

- an emphasis upon arts in the plural.
- a tendency to seek solutions to educational problems outside of the school proper.
- an inclination to involve community agencies as resource persons.
- a bias in favour of studio production/performance.
- a propensity for justifying arts education in terms of social and/or remedial enhancement.[74]

Certainly, when viewed in relation to the wider school curriculum, the arts do share many pedagogic elements, but there are problems with the clustered model of arts education, such as:

- The four arts may never be acknowledged as distinct disciplines in their own right. Each area offers a unique stage for encounters with self and episodes of disclosure.
- The clustered format creates its own form of curricular rigidity. For example, the arbitrary grouping of art, dance, drama, and music

education can lead students to erroneously assume that aesthetic and creative learning can only take place within the arts, as opposed to science or mathematics.

■ The clustered format continues curricular exclusion. For instance, language arts such as poetry and short stories are separated artificially from their next-of-kin within the clustered arts.

When confronted with the task of planning for clustered arts curricula, school administrators frequently incur the wrath of arts practitioners by deciding to (a) divide the time available equally among the four subjects, or (b) assign the whole time available to a single subject which they pencil in as "arts".

The former plan frustrates arts teachers because **the four-way time share usually leaves an insufficient amount of time to do any of the four areas properly.** The ensuing confrontation can be avoided, of course, by ensuring adequate amounts of time for all four arts subjects, but that requires pro-arts administrators who will take whatever steps necessary to find the extra time.

The latter decision creates dissension among arts teachers because, in reality, **there is no single subject called "arts".** What often passes for arts education is just a school musical under different billing. While the "*let's put on a show, I think my uncle has a barn we can use*" routine worked well for Mickey Rooney and Judy Garland, it is simply not an acceptable vehicle for the collective arts. The music students get to play music, the dancers get to dance, and the actors get to act. This leaves nothing for the artists to do but sit in the audience and applaud their classmates. In fairness, however, I should point out that the artists are usually allowed to paint the backdrops and print the tickets.

Art education and the performing arts

While all of the four subjects are unique and of equal educational value, it is important to acknowledge that art education usually stands apart from the performing arts, which include dance, drama, and music education. This situation is not always understood by school administrators, nor is it always acknowledged by arts educators, especially advocates of the arts-in-education movement. For example, Richard Courtney, a proponent of arts-in-education, offers the following *media-based theory of learning*:

Learning is the ability to use the skills of the media. It occurs, first, for expressive purposes and thereafter for critical purposes, so that the student can increasingly express his meanings to others. (Courtney, 1982, p. 11)

So far, so good. Courtney's theory certainly sounds inclusive. Art educators, however, will be dismayed to discover that the accompanying diagram *Figure 3: The Development of Media* (p. 11) contains only three learning strands:

a central line for drama, flanked by strands for music and dance. Apparently, art media do not contribute to learning.

To understand why art education is pedagogically distinct from the performing arts, we need to look closely at Courtney's notion of *the dramatic curriculum*:[75]

> Dramatic action serves a clear purpose in life. It is the prime mediator between our inner selves and the environment. It is a medium whereby our inner self works with the outer world and creates meanings out of it. Drama is a bridge, a filter, between the two worlds. (Courtney, 1982, pp. 5-6)

At the outset, Courtney's concept of dramatic action matches Rollo May's description of *creative courage*: both involve an encounter between the subjective self and the objective world. But drama becomes the "prime mediator" in Courtney's model due to his curiously limited notion of *Being*:

> For imaginings to become externalized, we need to act with them. When we are very young this is *to Be* - "I am an airplane." Once this is achieved, the child can extend the action to *elements* of Being: *to Sound* - "I make the sound of an airplane"; and *to Move* - "I make the movements of an airplane." (p. 8)

Courtney's three strands of "Being", which translate into drama, music, and dance education, share a common dependence upon corporeal action. For Courtney, "Being" requires a direct, bodily expression, in other words, a *performance*. What Courtney's model fails to acknowledge is that there is "no one way of being", to borrow a phrase from the title of his 1988 study into the practical knowledge of elementary teachers. "For imaginings to become externalized" we do not need "to act with them." We are not limited to pretending that we are an airplane, to sounding like one, or to moving like an airplane. We can *draw* an airplane or *construct* one, as well.

It is this lack of direct, corporeal action that separates art from the performing arts. Artists are not hanging in our galleries, nor do we usually see their activities in the studio. **Art is an indirect encounter between the subjective self and the objective world.** It might be worth noting at this point that art is not the only indirect arts discipline. The literary arts also function indirectly, and the *whole language process* closely parallels studio processes used in art education. School administrators wishing to cluster subject areas might well be advised to link art education with language arts rather than with the performing arts.

Direct and nondirect teaching in art

Having established that the performing arts operate directly and that art education functions indirectly, we can move to some of the pedagogic implications. In art education, "few teachers parallel the performance model of music and drama. Rather, most appear to have assumptions based on freedom of self-expression."[76]

The role of a classroom teacher in art education is rarely equivalent to that of a conductor or director in the performing arts. While secondary school art specialists sometimes assume the role of master artist and organize their studios as a kind of neo-guild shop with student apprentices, **the traditional teacher role in art education is that of a nondirective facilitator:**

> In most models of teaching, the teacher actively shapes events and can picture the pattern of activities that lies ahead; but in most nondirective situations, events emerge and the pattern of activities is more fluid. Second, from the teacher's point of view, counselling is made up of a series of responses that occur in an unpredictable sequence. Thus, to master nondirective teaching, teachers learn general principles, work to increase their sensitivity to others, master the nondirective skills, and then practice making contact with students and responding to them, using skills drawn from a repertoire of nondirective counselling techniques. (Joyce, Weil & Showers, 1992, p. 269)

Nondirective teaching is a frequently misunderstood form of professional practice. At the root of many misunderstandings is the mistaken belief that *teaching* is the same as *instruction*. Instruction is only a segment of the curricular sequence, whereas teaching refers to the entire pedagogic enterprise. **So when we speak of nondirective teaching strategies, we are not discounting the likely need for direct instruction at some point and for some duration. In art education, episodes of direct instruction are relatively brief and usually occur at the start of new projects.**[77] The majority of class time is spent on studio-based activities, which are nurtured most logically through nondirective strategies.[78]

Thus, while art teaching can be described as nondirective, there is no excuse for inadequate, or nonexistent, instruction: "Mere exposure to art is not enough. If it were, the most cultured members of society would be the guards in our art galleries and ushers in our concert halls."[79]

Integrating the arts

While Richard Courtney's media-grounded theory of learning cannot suffice as a model for arts education, numerous arts groups are currently working towards a more inclusive approach. One such group, the *Saskatchewan Arts Education Liaison Committee* (1991), has prepared organizing principles upon which all four arts subjects can be jointly planned:

■   The four strands of art, dance, drama, and music should be developed as discrete strands.

OMEA MODEL #1: THE MAJOR / MINOR FOCUS

	Major Focus	Minor Focus	
Strand A	MUSIC	ART	DRAMA
Strand B	ART	DRAMA	MUSIC
Strand C	DRAMA	MUSIC	ART

OMEA Model #1 describes a total arts offering in grade nine. It can be offered in any block of time designated for the arts but the major focus should be a minimum of two-thirds of the arts time allotment. If arts were offered every day of the week, the major focus would be taught for three days while the remaining two days would be devoted to the two minor areas. (OMEA, 1992, p. 23)

OMEA MODEL #2: THE MAJOR FOCUS / UNIFIED ARTS

ARTS FOCUS   UNIFIED ARTS COMPONENT

Music *or* Art *or* Drama

OMEA Model #2 also describes a total arts offering in grade nine. It can be offered in any block of time designated for the arts but the major focus should be a minimum of two thirds of the arts time allotment. If arts were offered every day of the week, the major focus would be taught for three or four days while the remaining time would be devoted to the unified (integrated) arts component. (OMEA, 1992, p. 24)

- The strands should be developed in three components: the creative/productive, the cultural/historical, and the critical/responsive component.
- The curriculum should be developed for use by both generalists and specialists.
- The required learning should include knowledge, skills, and attitudes.

There are four primary educational objectives upon which the integration of the four arts subjects can be justified: (a) dealing with the complexity of the world; (b) overcoming rigid perceptions of subject boundaries; (c) respecting the seamless web of knowledge; and (d) promoting greater efficiency.[80]

In a proactive response to Ontario's *The Common Curriculum, Grades 1-9*, the *Ontario Music Educators' Association* (OMEA) has devised two models of integration that could be used to implement the arts at the grade 9 level. It should be noted that the OMEA models do not include dance education because *at this time* it is not yet offered as a discrete course in most Ontario high schools.

Thus, through the preparation of organizing principles, the identification of educational objectives, and the presentation of working models for integration, arts educators are well on their way to dealing with the internal curricular competition that has so frequently slowed the maturation of arts education.

External competition from other school subjects

Art education has also been battered by external curricular competition from the wider array of school subjects. Such forces have struck at the very heart of art education, for they have brought into question two fundamental issues of *identity*: how do art educators wish to present themselves, and how do they hope to be seen? These two questions are really flip sides of the same coin and, as such, exist in a fluid state of symbiotic evolution.

Historically, art education has been viewed by the public with considerable apprehension. In its 1977 report, *Coming to Our Senses*, the Arts, Education and Americans Panel summed up public attitudes towards the fine arts:

- The fine arts were considered effete and unmanly by those frontiers people who valued rugged individualism (pp. 30-31).
- The arts were somewhat feared based on the belief they might have an unwholesome effect on the young and on traditionally held values (pp. 52-53).
- The fine arts had no practical application, a serious flaw for a business and profit-oriented populace.

- The fine arts were seen as the property of the wealthy and educated, not the "common man." The association of the arts with the elite conflicted with the home-spun values of independence and democracy. (p. 43).

Art does not appear do have gained much ground in recent years if Gallup Poll data are any indication:[81]

A recent Gallup Poll [Elam, 1990] on the American public's attitudes toward the public schools reported that in response to the question "what subjects would you require every public high school student who plans to go on to college to take," art and music ranked at the bottom of a list of fourteen at 24% (art) and 22% (music). The percentages were lower (17% and 16%) for those not planning to go on to college. (Pearse, 1992b, p. 85)

It is interesting to note that Gallup asks the American public to rate high school subjects in terms of their *value for college*, rather than their *value for secondary schooling*. This is not simply a question of semantics; the deliberate choice of "college" reflects the historical role played by universities in the selection and organization of high school subjects.[82] Art remains a low-status school subject for two basic reasons, both of which relate directly to post-secondary education: (a) it is not required for college entrance, and (b) it is not usually subjected to standardized testing.[83]

The results of pressures placed upon high school curricula by university specialists and committees are wholly predictable:

School subject groups tend to move progressively away from concerns with "utilitarian" or "relevant" knowledge. High status in the secondary school curriculum is reserved for abstract theoretical knowledge divorced from the working world of industry and the everyday world of the learner. (Goodson, 1987, p. 197)

Thus, **the road to curricular status follows a predetermined path, a path that steers school subjects clear away from any practical or social objectives.** Is it any wonder, therefore, that eloquent pleas which stress the existential value of art education prove to be unexpectedly counter-productive?

Perhaps the biggest impediment to improved public perception of the arts is the *inadequate preparation* preservice teachers receive in arts education.[84] Coupled with a conspicuous *absence of regulatory guidelines*, as well as the rapid *disappearance of specialists* at provincial, board, and class level,[85] generalist practitioners are prone to acquiring the *seasonal show-and-tell syndrome*:

Early in my administration career, I learned that a fine arts program could be annual PTA programs, colored turkeys and eight-year-old pilgrims at Thanksgiving, and a record

being played between 2:30 and 3:00 p.m. every Friday so
that the teacher could grade papers or clean off the desk.
Cranked-out rabbits and turkeys are *not* art education,
listening to records as a time killer is not music education,
and being a pilgrim does not a Thespian make. But these
scenes have the public eye and become, in a sense, a
curriculum of seasonal show and tell. (Cormack, 1991, p.
42)

Substantive reforms in art education

What "the public eye" has not seen, at least not clearly or frequently
enough, have been the substantive changes in art education over the past
decades. "Cranked-out rabbits" and "eight-year-old pilgrims" may not have
disappeared from our schools, but they are being supplanted by more
rigorous forms of art education:

Perhaps the reason why art education is placed at the
bottom of the list in parental priorities is that much of the
public does not know the new developments that have
evolved over the past few decades. The type of art
education that most people experienced in elementary
school probably fell into one of two categories: dictated art
or something called "creative self-expression."

The concept of art education has gradually evolved
so that current thought maintains that there is something to
learn in art, in addition to something to *express*.
(Herberholz & Hanson, 1990, pp. xxiii-xxiv)

Education is constitutionally not a federal responsibility in either
Canada or the United States, but **much of the impetus for curricular reform
has been generated by national art groups** in both countries. In 1991, U.S.
art, music, and drama groups issued the *National Arts Education Accord: A
Statement on Arts Education to Governors and State Legislators.* A
comprehensive but concise document, the *Accord* made arts-based
recommendations in areas as diverse as access, scheduling, teaching loads,
adult education, research, and religion.

In Canada, national art organizations have also worked, albeit
independently, to codify standards for art education. For example, the
Canadian Society for Education through Art (CSEA) has prepared a *National
Policy Position Statement* which recommends sweeping reforms to Canadian
art curricula.

At the 1990 CSEA Assembly held in Regina, Saskatchewan, Rita
Irwin chaired a panel discussion devoted to the assessment of provincial art
education experiences, 1980-90. In summary, she rallied the troops with the
following call to action:

CSEA NATIONAL POLICY POSITION STATEMENT

1. Art should be available in all schools at all levels.
2. Requirements for high school graduation should include at least one art course.
3. Curriculum must be formulated from theoretically sound, on-going research in the field of art education.
4. Instructional objectives must be formulated for all levels of teaching - elementary, secondary, and post-secondary.
5. A comprehensive set of teaching objectives should be defined.
6. The formulation of curricula should derive from a common core of learning, one which includes instruction in studio production, art criticism, and art history.
7. Canadian art education curricula should include national, regional, and local content.
8. Curriculum materials must be written by qualified specialists in the field of art education.
9. Instruction should be carried out by qualified art teachers.
10. Teacher education in the form of pre-service and in-service training should be made available for all teachers. (Baxter, 1987).

In review, the four foci for the 1980s could very well remain priorities for the 1990s. Provincial art education associations need to be political voices in good times and in bad times. Curriculum development initiatives need to support sequential programs seeking to balance studio activities, art history and art criticism. Teacher education, including preservice, inservice, and graduate work must become a high priority if we are ever to reach children and adults who are unaware of the value found in visual arts. Finally, we can feel strong about our accomplishments with galleries and the active use of their resources. We can also feel good about reaching very young children. However, again, we cannot sit back and accept that we have "arrived." Instead, we must reach for ever greater acceptance and understanding in these two domains of learning. (Irwin, 1992b, p. 45)

The emergence of art education has, indeed, been a tale of competition; but through its internal and external struggles, art has acquired a sense of *unity, integration*, and *identity*. And it is this growing sense of *collective self* that has helped many art teachers find the courage needed to teach.

3   Art in Theory

Extraordinary means are not necessary in order to achieve extraordinary ends, but that it is, rather, the skill with which ordinary thinking processes are used and the purpose to which they are put which enable outstanding results to be achieved. (p. 76)

Sharon Bailin (1988)
Achieving Extraordinary Ends:
An essay on creativity

Although the individual arts are unique subjects in terms of content, they share among them a common intent: the development of creativity in students. From this truism, however, two common educational misunderstandings emerge. First, many administrators assume that it is unnecessary to include all four arts in school timetables since art, dance, drama, and music expose students to the same epistemologic mode, namely, the acquisition of knowledge through creative exploration and disclosure. It is hoped that readers of this text will appreciate the innate value of art, dance, drama, and music, and convince administrators in their school districts to include all four art subjects in timetable plans.

A second misunderstanding, perhaps even more damaging to the education of students, can evolve from an undue emphasis upon the creative raison d'être of the arts. Educators can disassociate creativity from non-arts subject areas, especially mathematics and science. The Renaissance merger of arts and sciences can be lost to the misguided polarization of *arts versus science*. It is the spark of creativity that has allowed many great scientists to enter new realms of discovery and, similarly, artists have historically found inspiration through scientific study and the adoption of innovative media and processes.

3.1   Creativity

Although the development of student creativity is central to art education, the nature of creativity itself is often poorly understood by

creativity within assigned artistic activities, and devise assessment procedures which specify creativity as a criteria for evaluation. Yet, when asked by students or parents to define what they mean by creativity, these teachers are often unable to give even a cursory explanation. It is most important that practitioners possess a fundamental grasp of what creative processes can involve, and how they can be fostered through art activities.

Before we proceed, however, it should be clearly understood that this book is premised upon a belief that **all learners are capable of creative activities, not just those *born with talent*.** Admittedly, genetic and social conditions ensure that children enter school with visible proclivities and dispositions towards certain aspects of the curriculum and, yes, some youngsters will demonstrate greater affinity for art than others. The same holds true for young children who excel at arithmetic, spelling, or catching bean bags. It is the professional responsibility of teachers, however, to foster rudimentary levels of competence in their students across the curriculum, not just in areas that the students want to explore. Elitist notions of *artistic genius*[86] offer convenient excuses for generalist teachers who will not bother to acquire any art competencies, and specialists who only want to teach those students who can create intuitively. Of course, such teachers do their students a great disservice but, even more damaging, such educators fill our society with individuals unable to employ art in the task of coping with the stresses of modern life.

Given the central role of creativity within art education, it may come as a surprise to some that the nature of creativity remains hotly contested, even among art specialists. However, the diversity of opinion regarding creativity should be viewed as a strength rather than as a weakness. Explicit definitions and discrete boundaries, so crucial to logical inquiry within the sciences, can act as inhibitors to creative exploration within the arts. The range of artistic qualities held to be indicative of creative ability actually expands opportunities for student development within art curricula. Diversity is a cardinal rule within art.

For ease of discussion, our selection of historically significant theories of creativity will be presented using an overview adapted from Ridley (1969). In their broadest context, **theories of creativity can be considered to fall primarily within one of two conceptual frameworks: *creativity as behaviour* or *creativity as experience*. Proponents of the former concept view creativity as nothing more than a complex human behaviour, one that can be fully understood through the application of empirical behavioural analyses and replicated, applied, and modified within clinical settings. The opposing camp considers creativity to be a fundamentally process- rather than product-based phenomenon, fully understood only by individuals interacting directly and honestly with their personal environments.**

CREATIVITY AS BEHAVIOR

Group Ideation	Gordon
	Osborn
Elementarist	Dollard & Miller
	Flanagan
	Guilford
	Maltzman
	McPherson
	Mednick
	Torrance
	Wilson
Personality Assessment	Getzels & Jackson
	MacKinnon

CREATIVITY AS EXPERIENCE

Existential	Anderson
	Maslow
	May
	Rogers

Figure 3a: Theories of Creativity

(Adapted from Ridley, 1969)

The selected theories of creativity have been categorized in *Figure 3a: Theories of Creativity.* The listings are certainly neither exhaustive nor inclusive. No attempt has been made to discuss theories of creativity rooted in perspectives that are clearly not art-positive. Excluded, for example, are Freudian concepts of creativity which consider artistic activities to be little more than a socially accepted channelling of sublimated, unconscious desires. Purposely omitted, as well, are stimulus-response (S-R) behavioural theories[87] which ascribe creative actions (known to S-R proponents as *behavioural mutations*) to factors beyond personal control or modification:

> Skinner (1968) therefore denies any psychological trait called "creativity", because it implies personal, mentalistic control. It is creative *behaviours* that deserve attention, for being behaviours they must obey the same laws as do all others. They need not be mysterious or special merely because they are rare. But how do they come about? Purely by accident. Individuals seeking reinforcement via trial-and-error may sometimes emit *behavioural mutations*, unusual responses akin to those biological mutants that sometimes appear by chance in nature. (Abra, 1988, p. 73)

Creativity as behaviour

Behaviourist theories of creativity attempt to model or replicate creative processes through one of three approaches: *group ideation*, *elementarist* (or reductionist), or *personality assessment*. Proponents of creativity as behaviour have been traditionally found within the social sciences. Their efforts to supply scientific explanations for artistic phenomena dominated much of pedagogic literature during the 1950s and 60s. Despite promising early work, behaviourists have failed to produce any inclusive model of creative processes, and within art education the tide has gradually turned in favour of experiential notions of creativity.

Behaviourists traditionally researched creative processes by studying individuals in isolation. **Group ideationists, however, focused their attention upon interactions among individuals with the primary goal of identifying attitudes that encouraged and/or discouraged creative thinking**. Group ideation research targeted commercial and industrial employees and resulted in two processes still widely used within corporate circles today: *brainstorming*, developed by Osborn (1957), and *synectics*, introduced by Gordon (1961). The former technique relied upon deferred judgement as a method of fostering creative approaches to problem-solving. The latter theory, synectics, was purported to be a more complex form of brainstorming; its proponents claimed that perceptual biases were further reduced, thus tapping deeper cognitive strategies.

The majority of behaviouralist researchers, however, tried to reduce the innate complexity of creative actions by isolating creative elements from generic human behaviours. The singular elements, it was assumed, could then be subjected to scholarly, empirical testing with the expectation that an overall theory of creativity could be formulated, validated, and modified.

The idea that complex human behaviours could be understood through the study of isolated components produced theories of creativity that, when first proposed, appeared to be both simple and sensible.

Unfortunately, however, creativity is rarely simple, and often quite nonsensible. Ultimately, elementarist research proved to be incapable of providing a comprehensive theory of creativity.

To illustrate the limited value of elementarist research one can cite the deceptively simple notion, devised by Wilson (1951), that creative actions can be defined as "statistically infrequent behaviours." This empirical nomenclature, merely describing the concept of *creativity as originality*, typified the social science foundation of elementarist research. At first glance, Wilson's proposition seemed beyond criticism: who would argue against the need for artistic originality? Upon reflection, however, mere statistical infrequency within a given population sample did not suffice. Other researchers, such as Dollard & Miller (1950) and Maltzman (1960), insisted that creative solutions be linked to specified task situations; ideas had to be related to contexts, not merely be unexpected. Such amendments to Wilson's original approach produced the related concept of *creativity as utility*.

Other elementarist researchers conceptualized creativity as a process of linking apparently dissimilar concepts; the more remote the association, the more highly creative the linkage was rated. Proponents of *creativity as association*, such as Mednick (1962) and Flanagan (1963), developed pencil-and-paper tests that relied upon linguistic associations, an example of which was Mednick's *Remote Associations Tests (R.A.T.)*. These elementarists believed that high scores on linguistic associations would carry over into other subject areas and were evidence of overall creative ability.

Another avenue of research into creativity as behaviour, which also relied upon diagnostic tests, focused upon the factor analysis of personality traits. Researchers working within the concept of *creativity as personality trait* (Guilford, 1950, 1967) devised tests which included figural, semantic, and symbolic task situations. The tests were deeply criticized (Gruber, 1980; MacKinnon, 1967) for their inability to predict whether or not the allegedly creative potentials would actually be utilized or applied by individuals.

Elementarists who presented *creativity as artifact analysis* (McPherson, 1963) analyzed works of art for creative qualities in order to determine underlining creative processes. Research in this area became problematic when theorists were unable to distinguish between factors related to quantity and those related to quality.

Perhaps the most influential elementarist researcher was Torrance (1962) who conceptualized *creativity as task analysis*. He believed that the complex processes involved during creative acts depended upon four basic cognitive skills which he labelled fluency, flexibility, originality, and elaboration:

> Fluency refers to the ability to generate a large quantity of
> ideas, responses, solutions or questions. Teachers might ask
> students to list as many birds as they can or to list as many

different shades of green as possible. Flexibility is the ability to produce a wide variety of ideas, responses, solutions or questions and the willingness to change direction or to consider alternatives. For instance, a teacher might ask a child to consider how a turkey would view Thanksgiving dinner. Originality is the ability to produce unique and unusual responses. The teacher might ask how children would redesign a playground for children who are in wheelchairs. Finally, elaboration is the ability to add details to a given idea in order to expand upon it. Teachers might ask students how they could make a picture more interesting with the addition of more details. Encouraging fluency, flexibility, originality, and elaboration ultimately encourages students to toy with elements and concepts for themselves in a creative way. (Irwin, 1992a, p. 32)

Personality assessment also provided an avenue of research within the field of creativity as behaviour. Researchers working on personality assessment differed from group ideationists and elementarists in two fundamental ways: (a) they considered social contexts, and (b) they treated creativity as an integral part of human behaviour.

MacKinnon (1961) provided an operational model of creative behaviour which required: an element of originality; adaptation to contextual realities; a clear relationship to the original impetus; and, an ability to sustain itself during its integration with the social milieu.

Getzels & Jackson (1962) studied school and family units for potential social determinants of creativity. Although their studies were soundly criticized on methodological grounds, the inconclusive nature of their data proved to be even more problematic.

Creativity as experience

The preceding behaviourist concepts of creativity provided examples of how social scientists have sought to uncover the complex processes involved in creative thought. **Most artists, on the other hand, have approached creativity from an experiential perspective, and have stressed the importance of perceptual and cognitive styles over disparities among creative and less-creative individuals.** Most experiential notions do not lend themselves to empirical validation; proponents dismiss this weakness by suggesting that persons can validate such theories through reflection upon past experiences. This fundamental disagreement has maintained two solitudes within research into creativity, a state of disunity that weakens both approaches and retards progress within specific fields such as art education.

Proponents of creativity as experience can be classified within the single heading of *existentialists*:

> Creativity occurs in the moment of NOW, in the person whose openness to present experience is not disturbed by the taboos or expectations of others. ...Even though past experience and preparation are necessary for a creative act, the act can only occur in the open and truthful encounter with the environment. (Anderson, 1965)

This emphasis upon perceptual encounters with reality echoes previous positions by May (1969, 1975) and Schactel (1959). Maslow (1954, 1959a, 1959b) and Rogers (1961, 1970, 1982) also stressed these points, but they both emphasized the role played by interpersonal influences which, they contended, had the power to distort an individual's perception of reality.

The successful nurturance of creativity as experience in school settings requires educators to furnish an appropriately creative environment:

> Carl Rogers (1961) describes several conditions for constructive creativity which are consistent with contemporary philosophies held by early childhood classroom teachers. To begin, Rogers outlines three *inner conditions* which are necessary for the development of creativity: openness to experience, internal locus of evaluation, and the ability to toy with elements and concepts. (Irwin, 1992a, p. 31)

Taken together, these three cardinal principles describe an instructional setting that is key to art education: the *studio*. The pedagogic implications of studio education are detailed more fully within *Chapter 4: Art as Practice*.

Existentialists stress the importance of personal integrity during encounters with expressive media. Doyle (1971) claimed that practising artists saw honesty and artistic integrity as elements more central to their work than other features more traditionally given as criteria for creative expression, such as originality and craft. Doyle described how author Grace Paley used truth to edit her work; how poet Jane Cooper described her poetry as just a process of self-awareness; and how musician Joel Spiegelman found evaluating his own music difficult - it was just like looking at a mirror.

A novel resolution of the ongoing debate between proponents of creativity as behaviour and creativity as experience has been offered by Sharon Bailin, who suggests that neither of these polarized theories of creativity are valid:

> The contemporary view of creativity which has been the object of our scrutiny makes certain claims which form the basis for a set of educational practices aimed at fostering creativity. According to this view, there is a distinctive creative process of thought which is different from ordinary, logical thinking and which is characterized by the generation

of novelty, by leaps of imagination, by rule-breaking, and by irrational processes. Such processes are necessary in order to transcend the conceptual strictures of frameworks and to generate radical novelty. Being creative, then, involves possessing the cognitive and personality traits such as fluency, flexibility and non-conformity which make one good at the creative process, and is not necessarily connected with the production of products. (Bailin, 1988, p. 128)

Creativity, according to Bailin, is no different from ordinary rational though processes; it is little more than "excellent thinking and performing in an area."[88]   Unfortunately, however, Bailin goes on to suggest that creativity may be more than just skills, rules and rational processes, after all.   She admits that there is "something more" to creativity which could be expressed as "inspiration, illumination, vision, genius, to name only a few - but it is perhaps best captured by the concept of imagination."[89]   *Inspiration? Illumination? Vision? Genius? ...to name only a few?* It would appear that the debate continues, after all.

Clearly, it is not sufficient to simply tell students that you want to see creativity in art assignments. **It is critical that teachers think carefully about what they really mean by the term "creativity", and convey their expectations to students as explicitly as possible prior to the start of studio activity.**

The primary consideration centres upon whether one believes creativity to be essentially a behaviour, an experience, or both.   Creative behaviours result in external elements that can usually be monitored and assessed by the teacher. Creative experiences, on the other hand, produce internal elements that are best valued and understood by individual students. **Creative behaviours often lend themselves to quantitative assessments; creative experiences frequently involve qualitative descriptions.**

Some examples of appropriate *behavioural objectives* for art activities include:

- producing original work;
- devising useful solutions;
- finding relationships among similar or opposing elements;
- transforming ideas or relationships; and,
- manipulating artistic media to complement subject matter.

Some examples of appropriate *experiential objectives* for art activities include:

- self-motivation and absorption in work undertaken;
- reliance upon self for the resolution of artistic problems;
- clarity in explaining rationales for work undertaken;
- acceptance of constructive criticism from peers and teachers; and,
- willingness to undertake self-evaluation.

Before leaving the topic of creativity, some attention needs to be given to more generalized notions of human cognition, of which creativity is but one aspect. Some recent contributions to the field of cognition theory, which have significant value for arts education, include research into multiple intelligences[90] and brain hemisphericity.[91] Section 3.1 will conclude with discussions related to two perennial sources of pedagogic debate: the nature of skills acquisition and skills transfer.

Multiple intelligences

One of the most enduring public criticisms of contemporary education is the charge that schools fail to recognize or reward the diverse range of student abilities. This criticism centres upon the psychometric assertion that human intelligence is both stable and singular. The *belief in fixed intelligence*[92] has traditionally found wide acceptance within the field of education and large boards of education typically employ at least one educational psychometrist:

> The psychometric view regards intelligence as a *relatively stable* source of individual differences in the capacity for learning. As such, intelligence represents a construct posited to explain differences in learning - and *not* something that can be learned or taught in itself. In this pre-emptive way, intelligence is stipulatively defined as a general ability or aptitude (rather than an achievement) that *cannot* be either easily or greatly increased by instruction. Rather, intelligence functions as an external parameter that delimits instruction and partially explains differences in instructional outcomes. (McPeck, Martin, Sanders & Slemon, 1989, pp. 54-55)

For the most part, the notion that individuals have a relatively stable and predictable aptitude for learning seems to be true. Students who do well in English, usually do well in French; more often than not, such students excel in most of their academic subjects. Conversely, students who do poorly in school often fail most of their courses. In recent decades explanations for such phenomena have centred upon social determinants, such as socio-economic status, cultural capital, school preparedness, and various issues related to educational equity.[93] Traditionally, however, the predictability of pupil achievement has been accounted for in terms of cognitive theories, such as intelligence quotients (IQ), learning transfer, generic thinking skills, et cetera.

Critics of the psychometric view of fixed intelligence have long suspected that the predictability of student achievement is a reflection of the uniform epistomologic structure of academic subjects, rather than the uniformity of student aptitudes. Arts educator Howard Gardner has been working with the Rockefeller Foundation in an arts assessment programme called *Project Zero*:[94]

Program officers at the Rockefeller Foundation, our sponsors, felt that many young people are being cheated out of the opportunity to receive a good education - by college admissions criteria and so on - because, while they have many abilities and many achievements, they tend not to do well on standardized tests. There's a lot of agreement about that, even among the testing experts. Having a certain kind of intelligence we might call "test smarts" helps some people scoot through school very well, but everybody knows that it doesn't have nearly so much predictive value for what happens outside, or after, school. (Howard Gardner, *quoted in* Brandt, 1988, p. 33)

Project Zero sought to respond to the public's tacit belief that schools frequently fail to tap non-academic forms of student ability. Underpinning the Foundation's research into arts assessment was the *theory of multiple intelligences*:

Evidence from a variety of sources, especially new information about development of the nervous system and organization of the brain, indicates that human beings have evolved over a long period of time to think at least seven ways, which I call "intelligences." I mentioned two of them - mathematical and linguistic - but there's also musical, spatial, bodily-kinaesthetic, interpersonal, and intrapersonal intelligence. (Howard Gardner, *quoted in* Brandt, 1988, p. 34)

The theory of multiple intelligences offers an explanation for why students who do poorly in school often succeed later in careers that focus upon non-academic abilities. As well, the repeated emphases upon mathematical and linguistic forms of intelligence within most core academic subjects accounts for why students often perform equally well across a range of what are supposedly different courses. Finally, the reliance upon mathematical and linguistic abilities in psychometric tests and university entrance examinations explains why they are relatively reliable predictors of student academic aptitude.

The theory of multiple intelligences is clearly at odds with the established psychometric notion of a stable and singular form of human intelligence. Should Gardner's theory be true, and "the arguments and data are persuasive",[95] existing school curricula are failing to educate holistically; many of our present school dropouts may, indeed, be quite intelligent, after all. Clearly, curricular reforms based on multiple intelligences would place a greater emphasis upon arts education. Further, it should be noted that Gardner's listing of intelligences includes musical, spatial, and bodily-kinaesthetic forms; therefore, all four arts subjects would need to be emphasized within holistic curricula.

Brain hemisphericity

Similar calls for curricular reform have come from arts researchers working within the field of brain hemisphericity:

> The right brain - the dreamer, the artificer, the artist - is lost in our school system and goes largely untaught. We might find a few art classes, a few shop classes, something called "creative writing," and perhaps courses in music; but it's unlikely that we would find courses in imagination, in visualization, in perceptual or spatial skills, in creativity as a separate subject, in intuition, in inventiveness. Yet educators value these skills and have apparently hoped that students would develop imagination, perception, and intuition as natural consequences of a training in verbal, analytic skills. (Edwards, 1979, p. 37)

Medical studies conducted on split-brain patients[96] have demonstrated that **the two hemispheres of the brain not only house discrete functions, but process information differently**:

> It had long been known that the *functions* of the two hemispheres were different. Speech resides in the left brain and spatial capability in the right. But what was not known was that in *processing* information and stimuli, the left brain does a *lineal* type of processing, a sequential type, while the right brain uses a *global* process in which data is perceived, absorbed, and processed even while it is in the process of changing. (McCarthy, 1980, p. 71)

Specifically, left- and right-hemispheric processing characteristics differ in the following ways:[97]

Left-mode	*Right-mode*
verbal	nonverbal
analytic	synthetic
symbolic	concrete
abstract	analogic
temporal	nontemporal
rational	nonrational
digital	spatial
logical	intuitive
linear	holistic

For educators, such research has significant ramifications. First, teachers need to appreciate that there are two different *ways of knowing*, or learning.[98] **Learners begin by perceiving information, either by active sensory intuition, or by abstract intellectual reason. This is followed by processing information, which can be achieved either through active experimentation or by reflective observation.**

Second, educators need to accept that students differ in how they perceive and process information; **a variety of learning styles exist within any given student population, and should be given "equal time" within instructional activities.**[99]

Third, educators need to accommodate learning styles within overall school curricula and individual subjects:

> Even today, though educators are increasingly concerned
> with the importance of intuitive and creative thought, school
> systems in general are still structured in the left-hemisphere
> mode. Teaching is sequenced: students progress through
> grades one, two, three, etc., in a linear direction. The main
> subjects learners study are verbal and numerical: reading,
> writing, arithmetic. Time schedules are followed. Seats are
> set in rows. Learners converge on answers. Teachers give
> out grades. And everyone senses that something is amiss.
> (Edwards, 1979, p. 36)

Skills acquisition

Research into learning styles has resulted in curricular models such as Bernice McCarthy's *4MAT System*.[100] Typically, *4MAT* claims to be appropriate for the acquisition of skills in virtually any subject area. **Skills acquisition has traditionally been considered a linear phenomenon; students are taught fundamental rules or concepts, and then asked to apply the fundamentals within practical exercises.** *Discovery learning*, whether teacher-guided or not, is the flipside of the linear skills acquisition process; students begin with practical exercises, and are subsequently asked to derive fundamental rules or concepts.

The belief that skills acquisition is a linear process, where *"what to do in situation x"* is predicated on previously established rules or concepts, forms the basis for most pedagogic strategies; it reflects wider assumptions about cognition itself:

> According to Plato, all knowledge must be stateable in
> explicit definitions that any one can apply. If one could not
> state his know-how into explicit instructions - if his knowing
> *how* could not be converted into knowing *that* - it was not
> knowledge but mere belief. Cooks, for example, who
> proceed by taste, craftsmen who use intuition, poets who

work from inspiration, and prophets, like Euthyphro, who
preserve the tradition have no knowledge; what they do
does not involve understanding and cannot be understood
or taught. (Dreyfus & Dreyfus, 1984, p. 580)

Dreyfus & Dreyfus argued against this *information processing model of cognition*, which suggests that learning a skill is merely acquiring a step-by-step procedure.[101]   Their arguments were targeted specifically at researchers, such as Seymour Papert, who equated basic human cognition with computer-based approaches to *artificial intelligence* (AI):[102]

To let the phenomena of everyday, successful, skilled
activity show itself as it is, we will have to describe what the
tradition has passed over: what happens as one learns,
both from instruction and experience, to act appropriately
in a familiar domain. In attempting such a
phenomenological description we must be prepared to
abandon the traditional view that a beginner starts with
specific cases and, as he becomes more proficient, abstracts
and interiorizes more and more sophisticated rules;...It
might turn out that skill acquisition moves in must the
opposite direction: from abstract rules to particular cases.
(Dreyfus & Dreyfus, 1984, p. 582)

To illustrate their hypothesis that learning relies upon prototypes derived from personal experience, Dreyfus & Dreyfus have proposed a five-stage *model of skill acquisition*[103] using the simple, everyday context of learning to play cards.

The first stage, that of *novice*, involves the introduction of context-free facts and a few basic rules that provide the learner with a rationale for determining correct actions on the basis of the given facts.

In the second stage, that of *advanced beginner*, the basic rules are augmented with maxims that refer to situational aspects noted by the learner during drill-and-practice activities. It is important to note that even at this relatively early second stage the student begins to learn by prototype.

During the third stage, that of *competency*, the learner begins to adopt a hierarchical perspective on decision-making in order to cope with the overwhelming number of situational rules and maxims. A new feature appears at this point: unlike novices or advanced beginners, the competent performer feels responsible for his or her actions since they have become grounded upon personal perspectives or goals rather than upon de-contextualized rules and maxims.

The fourth stage, *proficiency*, involves a reduced reliance upon detached, conscious planning in favour of the intuitive identification of parallels between current situations and past experiences.

The final stage, *expertise*, sees the performer understand, act, and learn from the results without any conscious awareness of the process. The skill has become second nature.

The Dreyfus & Dreyfus model of skill acquisition challenges the widespread assumption that cognition is a linear construct, based upon the mastery of sequential steps; it proposes that "our everyday expertise is not "stored" in the mind of terms of facts and rules, at all, but in our memories of past situations already successfully confronted".[104] **The acquisition of skills, therefore, is an existential phenomenon activated by prototypical experiences grounded within personal perspectives.** Clearly, this model of cognition calls into question many current curricular and pedagogic structures; even more obviously, however, a model of skills acquisition through existential prototypes substantially validates contemporary arts education. Perhaps one of the best known Canadian proponents of such an approach to skills acquisition is Richard Courtney, whose text *The Dramatic Curriculum* explored the concept of learning through existential prototypes:

> Drama has grown steadily and surely throughout this century as a major way of learning. Many teachers have realized that the essential characteristic of human beings is their creative imagination - and that this is dramatic in style. Dramatic actions provide us with *meaning*: they make the things we do meaningful to us. Things do not have meaning by themselves. We give them meaning. Students in classrooms create meaning that is significant *to them*.
> (p. 4)

Skills transfer

The notion that school curricula need to be infused with existential meaning through dramatic, artistic, musical, or kinaesthetic experiences leads directly to the related issue of skills transfer: **Does existential exposure to arts education assist skills acquisition within other cognitive domains?**

Advocacy groups have argued that certain types of knowledge are superior to others on the basis of alleged educational transferability. Central to most arguments were the theory of *mental discipline* and the doctrine of *faculty psychology*:

> According to faculty psychology, the mind consisted of a series of discrete faculties that matured in response to particular sorts of training or cultivation. One conventional analogy was the development of the body through the exercise of different groups of muscles. A second metaphor was gardening. Teachers tilled or cultivated the pupil's mind with the aim of encouraging the growth of various moral and mental powers. The teacher's task was, for

example, to ensure that the faculty of memory was exercised, the moral faculties stimulated, the will disciplined, the reasoning powers improved, and the capacity for understanding strengthened. (Gidney & Millar, 1990, pp. 234-235)

Mental discipline and faculty psychology provided educators with curricular rationales that historically favoured Classical disciplines over the arts. It is ironic, given the demise of such theories in this century, to encounter remarkably similar arguments put forward by contemporary arts advocacy groups:

- The expressive arts foster "learning from the inside out," authentic learning that changes behaviour and encourages reflection.
- The expressive arts enhance the child's ability to interpret symbols.
- The expressive arts are associated with growth in all areas of development, including academics.
- The expressive arts regard the child as a meaning-maker and constructor, a discoverer and an embodiment of knowledge rather than a passive recipient of someone else's ready-made answers. (Jalongo, 1990, p. 196)

Certainly, arts educators endorse such claims for skills transferability. Unfortunately, however, advocates for other school subjects make disturbingly similar claims; we need only to substitute "expressive arts" for mathematics, science, physical education, et cetera.

Two issues arise from this situation. First, the similarity among the claims made by subject specialists has given impetus to the *generic skills* movement of the 1980s. While most educators no longer describe themselves as gardeners tilling fertile minds, the notion of mental faculties is still with us, albeit in the guise of generic skills.[105] **The cultivation of intellect still presupposes an element of transferability, not through the rigorous study of academic disciplines such as Latin, but through the resolution of "problems" that can be generalized.**[106]

Second, we need to clarify just how transferable skills really are. **Acquired skills can affect student learning in one of three ways: positively, negatively, or zero transfer.**[107] Assuming that we are concerned with ways in which the arts can act positively, we still need to distinguish between arts education as unique disciplines, and as methods of learning. Questions of learning transfer arise from the latter role and the ability of the arts to act as pedagogic methodologies for cross-curricular learning, apart from their roles as independent school subjects, is a recurring theme in this book. Whether we choose to employ the term *the dramatic curriculum* (Courtney, 1980) or emphasize the importance of *artistic disclosure* (Clark, 1987, 1990,

1991a, 1992a), the ability of existentially-based pedagogies to facilitate learning transfer is at the heart of many claims made by arts educators.

Courtney[108] has suggested that the following conditions are necessary to realize learning transfer:

- The similarity between the tasks must be maximized.
- There should be adequate experience with the original task.
- A variety of examples should be provided when teaching concepts and principles. Important features of a task should be identified and, perhaps, labelled.
- The teacher must ensure that general principles are understood before expecting much transfer.

Subject advocates need to ensure these fundamental conditions are in place before any claims to learning transfer are made.

3.2   Aesthetics

The development of creativity in students is not a question of the quantity of artifacts produced nor the frequency of their production; rather, it involves the quality of artifacts and the artistic experiences that produced them.   Students and teachers, therefore, must possess a practical understanding of how artistic experiences can be discussed qualitatively:

> Young children need regular opportunities to describe what
> they see, to react to works of art with their own feelings,
> and to reflect upon a variety of interpretations found within
> works of art. Early childhood is the time to begin laying an
> aesthetic foundation. Children at this age level can begin
> to notice pleasing relationships, for instance, between
> colours, textures, and lines. They can also come to identify
> a great variety of materials artists use: paints, musical
> instruments, props for assuming roles; and a great variety
> of styles: realistic or imaginary visual images, classical violin
> or fiddle melodies. As children respond to works of art
> with their developing attitudes, beliefs, values, and feelings,
> discussions will help them to sharpen their perceptual and
> sensory awareness and, thus, positively influence their own
> artistic productions. (Irwin, 1992a, p. 27)

We are talking now about aesthetics, about dealing with questions of *artistic value*. The field of aesthetics is often limited to Classical notions of *beauty*, however, our discussion of aesthetics will extend beyond questions of mere artistic beauty to the those of artistic value.

For teachers uncomfortable with the diversity of approaches to creativity, the prospect of dealing with the subjective field of aesthetics may well prove overwhelming. It is, however, the implicit divergency of aesthetics that necessitates its inclusion in sound art curricula. Through aesthetic discussions, students begin to rely on *self* to understand and respond to others around them. They learn to look inside themselves and discover artistic values that provide answers to the primary question, "*Who am I?*" With sufficient practice in aesthetic activities, students become more articulate and purposeful in their selection of personal effects that relay to the external world, "*This is who I am.*" As young adults in later life, they will be able to constructively employ aesthetic elements in the creation of environments at home and at work that harmonize with their inner selves.

The discovery of self and its positive integration within the social milieu provide teachers with two of their most crucial tasks. Art does not possess a monopoly on the development of self within students; ideally, all parts of the school experience contribute to this fundamental process. The emphasis within art upon divergent pedagogies, however, provides educators with an especially fertile ground for the nurturance of self.

The notion that aesthetic experiences form the core of arts education is steadily gaining wider acceptance. The performance emphasis, which traditionally provided most arts curricula with a *make-and-take* or a *let's-put-on-a-show* perspective, is gradually giving way to lifestyle activities geared towards the general population. Not many of our students will have etching presses in their homes, nor will their neighbourhoods likely provide a local repertory theatre. Although they will be encountering the arts throughout their adult lives, such events will require the appreciation of aesthetic values, not the performance of artistic skills. They will be listening to music, not playing instruments; they will be viewing art, rather than manipulating media.

The increasing popularity of new art curricula grounded in aesthetics, such as *discipline-based art education* (DBAE),[109] will require art teachers to develop a repertoire of pedagogic skills within the area of aesthetic education. But before such skills can be developed, educators must familiarize themselves with the dominant theories of aesthetics.

As with the previous discussion of creativity, the theories presented in the following pages provide an historic overview of key figures in the field of aesthetics and brief descriptions of the concepts each has contributed. Much effort has been made to reduce the amount of art- and aesthetics-related jargon to a bare minimum. *Figure 3b: Theories of Aesthetics* presents historically significant theories associated with both camps.

Theories of aesthetics, like those of creativity, can be discussed within two broad categories: *aesthetics as experience* or *aesthetics as response.* **Aesthetics as experience theories focus upon the activities of artists during acts of creation.** The percipients (viewers) are the individual artists, and their experiential phenomena are primarily focused within the domain of sensation. Assessments of experiential activities are conducted subjectively by the artists involved.

AESTHETIC RESPONSE

Cognition-Objective	Bell
	Broudy
	Eisner
	Fry
	Smith
Emotion-Subjective	Aristotle
	Bullough
	Kierkegaard
	Read
	Santayana
Combination	Bergson
	Chandler
	Dewey
	King
	Tolstoy

AESTHETIC EXPERIENCE

Phenomenological	Denton
	Heidegger
	Husserl
	Kasson
	Van Manen

Figure 3b: Theories of Aesthetics

(Adapted from King, 1981)

Aesthetic response refers to human behaviour towards works of art or artistic activities viewed externally by those other than the artist, whether they be naturally-occurring or produced. Aesthetic responses may be either pre-reflective or reflective. The percipient is always the individual observer, however, that person is considered primarily as a member of a group or of society-at-large. During episodes of aesthetic response, up to three domains may be at work: *cognition, emotion,* or *both.*

Ultimately, our valuing of art rests on how we are affected by a work. Yet the possibility for such aesthetic response is closely connected with the kinds of factors previously outlined. It is knowledge related to technique, style, and artistic context that opens up possibilities for appreciation which go deeper than a pre-critical response; and it is factors relating to the climate of the time that inform the sensibility of an era, affecting what will speak to and touch an audience, and thus what will be appreciated and valued. (Bailin, 1988, p. 44)

Aesthetics as response

Responsive theories may be centred within one of three domains: *cognition, emotion,* or a *combination* **of cognition and emotion.** The domains do not exist as discrete entities but as a continuum along which any response can be roughly positioned.

Cognitively-based theories of aesthetic response demand pre-requisites of the percipient, or viewer, such as: dispositions, expectations, analytic skills, studio proficiencies, et cetera. These responses involve cognitive interaction with aesthetic elements based upon objective criteria and logical reasoning. Eisner (1972), author of the *theory of selective response,* started with the premise that what we know determines how we respond and has suggested six frames of reference that could be brought to the contemplation of an aesthetic artifact:

Experiential	response focused upon how one is affected by the work
Formal	how the work is structured physically or compositionally
Symbolic	meanings of symbolic elements affecting the viewer
Thematic	ways the theme is comprehended by the viewer
Material	application, arrangement, and dynamics of the media
Contextual	nature of the environment in which the work is found

Other cognitive frameworks include the *thrill concept* developed by Bell (1958) and Fry (1956). The thrill concept is a theory of aesthetic response that seeks to duplicate the process-based phenomena contained within aesthetic experience. Viewers are expected to recreate, through the proper identification and sequencing of the aesthetic elements signalled by the work of art, the thrill that was originally experienced by the artist. Broudy (1976) describes three stages of cognitive response: innocent, conventional, and cultivated (p. 90). Cultivated aesthetic response allows the viewer to discern root metaphors and archetypical images within works of art. Smith (1970) also offers a three-stage model of cognitive response: aesthetic enjoyment, aesthetic particularity, and aesthetic knowledge (p. 61).

Emotion-based theories of aesthetic response can be traced to ancient philosophers, such as Aristotle, who sought to account for the impact that tragedy had upon the audience in Classical Greek theatre. Aristotle described the viewers' response, to a dramatic form of aesthetics, as an interval of emotional purging which he termed *catharsis*.

Other important emotion-based theories include:

Aesthetic response as empathy (Read, 1943)

Self-identification with elements within the artifact.

Aesthetic response as objectified pleasure (Santayana, 1959)

Beauty as the manifestation of sensory or emotional joy.

Aesthetic response as psychic distance (Bullough, 1959)

Cognitive or emotional distance between viewer and artifact.

Aesthetic response as sensuous immediacy (Kierkegaard, 1959)

A sense of sensory oneness with the artifact by the viewer.

The third category of aesthetic response requires reactions from percipients that involve cognitive and emotional elements:

Intuition as aesthetic union (Bergson, 1911)

Similar to Kierkegaard's notion of sensuous immediacy, aesthetic union is the result of subjective intuition.

Intuition as cultural validation (Tolstoy, 1959)

Proponents of objective intuition maintain that the values or beliefs of society-at-large determine the associational elements operational during aesthetic response.

Transitional response (Dewey, 1916)

Dewey believed that aesthetic responses began with emotional elements resulting from experiential *learning by doing*; the subsequent cognitive stage emerged as a result of contexts provided by the production of artifacts.

Associational response (Chandler, 1966)

Chandler suggested that percipient response may take the form of four modes of personal association with the work. For example, associational responses to a sculpture might include:

i   the *objective* viewer, who could say that the sculpture was too tall;

ii   the *intra-subjective* viewer, who could say that he could not touch the sculpture;

iii   the *associate* viewer, who could say that the sculpture reminded her of a bird in flight; and,

iv   the *character* viewer, who could say that the sculpture was too sad.

Before leaving our overview of aesthetic response, it might be worthwhile to see how some of these historically significant theories have developed in more recent years (Weltzl-Fairchild, 1991). Horner (1988) has produced a transitional model which begins with an internal, subjective phase and proceeds to an external, objective phase. Horner's sequence of aesthetic response, emotional to cognitive, is similar to John Dewey's model, however, the stages within each of Horner's response phases incorporate the postmodernist notion that the aesthetic elements embedded within the artifact are modified by what the percipient brings to the experience (see Eisner's theory of selective response):

Aesthetic Response, Horner (1988)

Phase One: **Internal Response**

Forgetting   entering into a fusion with the work
Remembering recalling the journey into the work
Reflecting   thinking about the whys of the journey
Revealing   becoming aware of one's desires, fears

Phase Two: **External Response**

Describing   decontextualizing the parts of the work
Structuring   noting the patterns of space and time
Interpreting   becoming aware of the social discourse
Retro-activating assessing the experience contextually

Another recent developmental model of aesthetic response by Parsons (1986) focuses primarily upon cognition since "cognitions give shape to emotions and for that reason are the better focus for developmental analysis" (p. 108):

Aesthetic Response, Parsons (1986)

Favouritism
Paintings are experienced as direct stimuli of pleasure, particularly their colour and subject matter.

Subject
Realism of the subject is the important consideration. Certain subjects are rejected on idiosyncratic moral grounds.

Expression
Paintings are understood as metaphors for ideas and emotion and are valued for the emotions they inspire. A distinction is made between the viewer's feelings and those in the painting.

Medium/form/style
Consideration of the artist's intent is important. Style is a carrier of historical thought and feeling and has public significance. Knowledge of these is more important than the feelings evoked.

Judgment
The personal meaning a painting elicits is weighed within the tradition to which it belongs. This is an ongoing process of testing the values of society and those of the viewer.

Aesthetics as experience

Aesthetic experience is process-centred; attention is not focused upon the artifacts produced but rather upon the qualities of the activity

itself. Researchers within the field attempt to understand the essences of such activities, not the facts of the resultant artifacts. Groups engaged in such field research often include psychologists and some philosophers, though the dominant perspectives within the field are provided by individuals known collectively as *phenomenologists*. The founder of modern phenomenology was Edmund Husserl who conceived the fundamentals of *phenomenological reduction*, or *bracketing*:

> We put out of action the general thesis which belongs to the essence of the natural standpoint, we place in brackets whatever it includes respecting the nature of Being: this entire natural world which is continually "there for us", "present to our hand", and will ever remain there, is a "fact-world" of which we continue to be conscious, even though it pleases us to put it in brackets. (Husserl, 1913, p. 110)

The phenomenological inquiry approach involves four levels, or types, of reduction:[110]

- activating one's interest in questioning the essence of world experience;
- overcoming subjective feelings, preferences, inclinations, or expectations;
- stripping away theories or scientific conceptions that condition how we typically experience phenomena; and,
- moving beyond the particulars of a lived experience to see its universal essence.

Denton (1979), has developed three modalities of bracketing:

Cognitive Bracketing
The conscious, pre-reflective act of setting aside accustomed perceptual sets and interpretive frameworks;

Existential Bracketing
Fresh perceptions appear due to an interruption in the normal flow of events, such as an unexpected death.

Dramaturgical Bracketing
In this form of bracketing, art processes are used to set aside familiar perspectives, to facilitate the acceptance of new perceptions, judgements, and interpretations. Denton's dramaturgical bracketing is a specific example of the *aesthetic world* or *play world* used by Heidegger (1962) to contrast the ordinary *mundane world*.

Phenomenologists speak of the *lived experience*; experience that is conscious but pre-reflective. Max van Manen (1990, 1991) offers the analogy of teachers being aware that the students are "looking at you" during lessons.[111] Cheryl Kasson (1981) prefers to stay within the lived experience as she observes phenomenologically, rather than segmenting each of the sequences into fragments that require special skills for analysis and/or perception.

Although considerable effort has been taken to simplify the complex strands of aesthetic theory and to reduce jargon to an absolute minimum, the task of integrating aesthetic education into art curricula may still seem overwhelming. Upon reflective second reading, however, it is hoped that the bedrock foundation of common sense underpinning the various theories will emerge. Aesthetic education is not really that mysterious nor is it really that unfamiliar. Consider the following basic points:

■   Aesthetic activities simply involve making qualitative judgments about artistic value; such decisions are made by ordinary people many times each day.

■   One way to engage aesthetic sensibilities is through direct participation in artistic processes.

■   A more prevalent method of developing aesthetic skills involves responding to artistic works produced by others. Aesthetic responses may take the form of carefully thought out analyses, gut reactions, or a combination of both.

The next step involves designing art curricula using these points. Aesthetic sensibilities engaged though participation in artistic processes are developed whenever students draw, paint, print, or sculpt. **Experiential aesthetic episodes are internal and require student-centred pedagogic strategies**, such as:

■   giving open-ended assignments that encourage the exploration and expression of self;

■   avoiding direct interventions during artistic activities, such as drawing the nose for a student's portrait;

■   using proper art terminology when talking to students about their work, and expecting the same in return;

■   discouraging students from seeing teachers as their primary sources of direction or evaluation; and

■   fostering student appreciation for artistic processes, as well as the production of artifacts.

External clues which suggest that students are experiencing aesthetic processes include: a sense of student ownership of the assignment, on-task behaviours, clarity in rationalizing work-in-progress, and an intuitive awareness of when work is done.

Developing student skills in the area of aesthetic response is pedagogically easier because the activities are external and, therefore, more

readily controlled by the teacher. The best way to initiate aesthetic responses is to ask the students to discuss their own work. All too many teachers erroneously assume that aesthetic activities only occur in response to great works of art. In reality, most young students are ill-equipped to appreciate or even understand works done by artists from differing cultures centuries ago.[112]

To compensate for weak art backgrounds and intellectual immaturity, teachers often tell students how they ought to respond, resulting in boring episodes of rote memorization or factual regurgitation. Art teachers can avoid this situation by encouraging students to respond at their own level, thus enriching and moderating inappropriate adult standards and expectations:

> In Taunton's (1986) investigation of the development of aesthetic values among children in grades one through three, her analysis of peer interaction and of conversations between students and their art teachers revealed ten kinds of standards being used when art works were discussed. Some standards, such as attention to detail and uniqueness of expression, were emphasized by teachers. Other standards, such as those relating to children's peer culture of their fascination with strange subject matter, originated from the students. It was apparent that both the teachers and students were determining the standards for art work completed in class, and students were aware that at times their criteria differed from those of their teachers. (Kakas, 1991, p. 23)

A good approach, for which most students have a chance of success, involves aesthetic responses to the artistic value of works familiar to young learners: *The Simpsons*, the latest video by Madonna, a Stephen King novel, or better still, their most recent class project. Such discussions can begin with emotional responses that require minimal reflection: "I liked the painting because the ballerinas were so graceful." With further practice and confidence, students can be more specific in their responses: "I selected *Sunday Afternoon on the Island of La Grande Jatte* by Seurat because I am fascinated with his pointillist technique." The six *frames of reference* developed by Eisner could provide a sound curricular foundation for the inculcation of aesthetic sensibilities; they can be applied to student projects as easily as to great works of art. As they mature, students should be given opportunities to respond aesthetically within a variety of curricular contexts: self-evaluations, peer critiques, and class discussions. Finally, it should be noted that a balance ought to be maintained between verbal and written aesthetic response activities.

Karen Hamblen and Camille Galanes (1991) have proposed six different instructional approaches to aesthetic education:

Historical-philosophical approach
Treats aesthetics as a traditional academic subject. The abstract nature of most aesthetic theories makes this strategy unsuitable for many students, especially young children.

Cultural literacy approach
Is currently a popular method of applying aesthetic knowledge and skills to a wide range of contemporary media. Students are required to recognize major artists, styles, techniques, movements, and exemplars of great works of art (usually male and Eurocentric).

Aesthetic inquiry approach
Depends primarily upon high-order thinking skills, and functions within language rather than studio. Arguments based upon logic, rationality, or persuasiveness are applied to what has been "said about art", rather than derived from the art objects themselves.

Social-critical consciousness approach
Examines art works for imbedded value statements, especially those that reflect class- and gender-based orientations. This method is often favoured by curricular reconstructionalists.

Cross-cultural/multi-cultural approach
Stresses the diversity of artistic activity. This method can involve humanistic, formalistic, or populist strategies.

Perceptive/experiential approach
Links aesthetics with traditional studio activities. By working directly with art forms, students develop a natural aesthetic sensitivity.

When deciding which of these instructional approaches to use, teachers need to be aware of their own academic backgrounds, their traditional teaching styles, and the abilities of their students.

3.3   Artistic activity

One of the most enduring topics for discussion among art educators involves the question of *product versus process.* In reality, however, there is no choice to be made: sound art curricula respect the value of both process and product. It is difficult to imagine how one can regularly obtain good products without a reliance upon good processes; similarly, just how good can processes be if they don't result in good products? Process and product are simply not mutually exclusive entities.

The art as process position is exemplified in typical elementary school curricula where art activities are seen as pedagogic methodologies for the development of generic social and academic skills.[113] This rationale for process-based art curricula in elementary schools has been validated by educational theorists such as Dewey and Montessori, and art specialists such as Lowenfeld & Brittain and Read. Process-based art curricula are usually referred to in the literature as *education through art.*

The public has been persuaded to support art curricula at the secondary level, however, through arguments grounded in the notion of art as product. Indeed, art was introduced into most North American educational systems in the guise of *drawing.*[114] At first, product-based art curricula in secondary schools were designed to provide skilled draughtsmen for the industrial workforce circa 1900. By the turn of the century, however, art curricula in secondary schools began to focus upon cultural and aesthetic concerns, the roots of which can be found within the *accomplishments curricula* designed for girls in the late 1800s.[115] Product-based art curricula are usually described as *education in art*, and they can be found most frequently within secondary level academic or vocational programs.

Thus, the product versus process debate has produced two streams of art curricula: education through art, and education in art. Clearly, **if we wish to construct a coherent continuum for art from kindergarten to grade 12 we must provide conceptual frameworks that rely on constructs other than product or process.** Two conceptual frameworks are needed: (a) one that explores the nature of artistic activity and (b) another that identifies a curricular phenomenon common to a wide variety of art curricula.

One of the fundamental reasons that elementary and secondary art curricula remain as two solitudes is the assumption held by many educators that one (meaning *their*) form of artistic activity is be superior to all others. **Rather than expending energy in the defence of one particular form of** artistic activity, art teachers should be seeking a conceptual framework that is inclusive and responsive to the curricular realities in which art operates. The following typology of artistic activity meets both of these criteria and consists of three modalities of artistic activity: private, public, and popular.[116]   This triadic typology of artistic activity is an example of *postmodernist* art education:

> Within the past fifteen years a critical writing in literary theory, art history and criticism, social theory, and more recently, art education research has identified a style referred to as *postmodernism*. Postmodernism describes a situation in which art includes popular, commercial, ethnic and other cultural forms, as opposed to an exclusively fine or high art deriving from the western European Renaissance. However, this widespread change in thinking does not appear to have significantly changed classroom art practice in elementary and secondary schools. There, for the most part, the dominant cultural bias is still Renaissance-influenced and technically based. (Abrahams, 1986, p. 64)

Private art

The focus of artistic activity undertaken by an individual in isolation is therapeutic by nature. The term therapeutic is *not* being used here within the context of the psychological discipline of art therapy, wherein children's artifacts are treated as projective devices to be subjected to analyses by clinical psychologists; rather, it is used within the context of actions taken in relation to the positive nurturance of self.

The impulse for such an activity is a desire originating from within the individual to be purged of built-up emotional energy. The impulse may be sparked by positive or negative emotions. In either case, a cathartic release signals the completion of the activity; cathartic release being defined as a purification or purgation of inner emotions.

The modality of private art, therefore, corresponds closely to Aristotle's description of the impact that tragedy had upon the audience in ancient Greek theatre; in both situations, a cathartic release is sought by the individual. While catharsis is an internalized, affective phenomenon, its progress can often be traced through the observation of external, physical actions.

It is important to keep in mind that the primary product of private artistic activity is an internal catharsis. The artifact produced is only a vehicle used by the individual in order to obtain emotional catharsis; it is not the end product itself.

Since private artistic activity is by nature internal, its validation or assessment should be conducted by the individual concerned. The relative success or value of the activity can only be described in terms of the degree of cathartic release.   Should frustrations or unsatiated energies remain unexpressed, the activity would be described as having been relatively unsuccessful.

Private art is primarily emotion-based; therefore, the fundamental requirement for participation in such activity is attitudinal. The individual must be willing to acknowledge the existence of internal emotions needing expression and to respond accordingly.

Public art

The focus of artistic activity undertaken by an individual within a group environment is aesthetic by nature. The impulse for engagement in such an activity is a desire within the artist to communicate some aesthetically-based message to others.

The product of public artistic activity is a communicated message disclosed by the artist. The disclosed information is both internal and external.   First, there is a concrete artifact produced which provides a physical manifestation of the message.   Secondly, there is a conceptual element that represents the internal thoughts disclosed by the individual to the wider group.

The validation of public artistic activity lies with the group, not the artist. Obviously, the group must be speaking the same language as the artist; that is to say, the group must be aesthetically literate enough to perceive the disclosed message contained within the artifact. Groups unable to demonstrate this capability are unfit for evaluative roles.

The requirements for public art include:

- A literate recipient, or group of recipients, willing and able to respond aesthetically to the disclosed information. Thus, the group requirements are both attitude- and ability-based.
- A trained artist, willing and able to aesthetically disclose personal messages to the group. Thus, the requirements of the individual are also both attitude- and ability-based.

Popular art

The focus of artistic activity undertaken by an individual on behalf of a cultural or social unit is utilitarian by nature. By utilitarian, it is meant that the activity occurs within a social milieu and that it serves a predefined purpose determined not by the artist but the social unit.   Industrial and commercial applications of art are examples of popular art.

The product of popular art is an artifact. The intent and content of the artifact are reduced to their bare essentials so that they can be understood by the relevant social unit, which is composed of both aesthetically literate and illiterate persons. Occasionally, popular art may be directed towards a specific sub- segment of society; under such conditions, the aesthetic elements employed may be more sophisticated and, therefore, unintelligible to other social groups.

The validation of popular artistic activity is conducted by the cultural or social unit for which it was produced. Degrees of success achieved are related to the breadth of consensual agreement with, and comprehension of, the artifact within the social unit.

The universality of the aesthetic components of popular art reduces the status of the artist to that of a technician. The requirements, therefore, for participation in popular artistic activity are ability-based. The communicative content is provided by the social unit and is deliberately uni-dimensional so that the public-at-large can decode the message. Little attitudinal input, therefore, is necessary from the artist.

Adoption of this typology of artistic activity would reduce the degree of energy expended by art educators in the defence of one specific modality of artistic expression over others. For example, the ongoing debates concerning the relative merit of *applied arts versus fine arts* or *low art versus high art* would finally be put to rest; in each case, the former modality would find its validation within popular art, and the latter within public art. Similarly, arguments related to the value of artifacts produced by children or untrained artists,[117] as well as existential notions of creativity and aesthetics could find resolution within the notion of private art.

The notions of private, public, and popular art are not new, and attempts at inclusion have been tried, such as the Weimer-era *Bauhaus School*:

> The Bauhaus was intended to reinstate the social and artistic virtues of the so-called "lesser" arts - the crafts, architecture, industrial and design arts. It sought to get away from the romantic social notion of the "pure" painter or sculpture as privileged and heroic, and instead to carry on William Morris' ideal that "the best artist was a workman still, and the humblest workman was an artist".
> (Abrahams, 1986, p. 64)

Still, however, there is no singular, accepted notion of artistic activity, and attempts to identify one have only lead to debilitating schisms within the field of art education. Similarly, attempts to demonstrate the superiority of art over music, music over drama, et cetera have only wasted time and energy, two educational resources in chronic short supply. Hopefully, the adoption of this more inclusive typology of artistic activity will allow arts educators to be more supportive of each other, and to better serve the students in their schools:

> The history of past movements is strewn with the wreckage of foiled attempts at reform, and the error has been the tendency to limit forms of thought to those found in one stream to the exclusion of the other. The task of general education, and art education within it, will not be served by separating living thought from feeling and action, as has been the case throughout the century, but by giving play to all the forms of engagement through which reality may be experienced and understood. (Efland, 1990b, p. 133)

3.4   Artistic disclosure

The second conceptual framework needed for the construction of a kindergarten to grade 12 art continuum centres upon the identification of a curricular phenomenon that is common to a wide variety of art curricula. Clearly, neither product nor process have succeeded in providing such a unifying curricular commonality, despite decades of determined efforts by proponents of each to design art curricula emphasizing product or process. The enduring popularity of product- and process-based activities suggests, however, that any alternative curricular phenomenon put forward should incorporate elements of both modes of activity.

Perhaps the simplest, and therefore the most overlooked, commonality among the vast array of art activities within school curricula is this: students are disclosing information within the artifacts that they are producing.

Self-disclosure was a concept introduced in 1958 by psychologist, Sidney Jourard (1958, 1971). In layman's terms, self-disclosure referred to the kinds of information that individuals were willing and able to share about themselves to others. This threshold of openness played important roles in group therapy techniques, as well as in individual psychoanalysis.

Whenever students engage in artistic activities, they give physical form to previously invisible thoughts. In doing so, the students disclose information to those around them. **If they give form to thoughts that are primarily personal,** *self-disclosure* **occurs; if their artifacts reflect primarily the thoughts of others,** *cultural-disclosure* **takes place** (Clark, 1987, 1990, 1991a, 1992a). These patterns of disclosure are not discrete; reflecting the inter-relatedness of self and culture, they often overlap and enrich individual acts of student disclosure.

It would seem prudent at this point to distinguish between student disclosure and student expression. In terms of art, student expression is inextricably linked to the romantically- based pedagogy of *creative expressionism*. Pioneered by 20th-century educators such as Frank Cizek,[118] creative expressionism espouses the belief that children spontaneously develop artistic skills according to natural laws; it is the antithesis of the contemporary pedagogy of discipline-based art education. One of the major goals of disclosure-based curricula is a bridging of the gulf between the promotion of art as process (education through art) and art as product (education in art). Thus, **it was necessary to use a linguistic construct other than expression to denote a more deliberate approach to artistic activity, one that reflected process as well as product, an approach that recognized the need for expressive precision within studio production:**

> The rules of performance in the arts, internalized as skills, are crucial for artistic achievement. Such skills are not a matter of blind and automatic performance, but involve considerable thought, flexibility, and the constant possibility of revision. Thus it is the mastery of such skills which allows one the freedom to go on and to make significant contributions. (Bailin, 1988, p. 105)

Disclosure was selected to achieve this subtle but crucial nuance and was meant to convey forms of student artistic activity that contained differentiated levels of both product and process, ability and attitude.

Chapter 1 began with the assertion that creativity requires courage. According to Rollo May, such courage is needed whenever individuals engage in encounters with the subjective self and the objective world. Our concept of disclosure, with its differentiated levels of both product and process, ability and attitude, provides a good fit with May's objective- and subjective-grounded notion of creative courage.

Disclosure can also provide a sound curricular foundation for *confluent models of art education*:[119]

> Essentially, confluence education is a melding of the affective domain (feelings, attitudes, values) with the cognitive domain (intellectual knowledge and problem-solving abilities). This approach adds the affective component to the conventional subject matter curriculum that is already in place. Those who support this design do not favour either content or experience or intellect or feeling; rather, they strive to blend the subjective or intuitive with the objective. (Ornstein & Hunkins, 1993, pp. 254-255)

At this point, our kindergarten to grade 12 art continuum can be constructed. It will rely upon the two principal forms of disclosure as its unifying curricular phenomena: self- and cultural-disclosure. As well, it will incorporate the earlier conceptual framework of private, public, and popular artistic activity. This K-12 art continuum is charted within *Figure 3c: Role of Disclosure within Art Education.*

	Elementary	Academic Secondary	Vocational Secondary
Programme	Integrated Arts	Fine Arts	Applied Arts
Modality	Private Art	Public Art	Popular Art
Disclosure	Self	Self	Cultural
Focus	Therapeutic	Aesthetic	Utilitarian
Referent	Individual	Group	Society

Figure 3c: Role of Disclosure Within Art Education

(Clark, 1987, 1990, 1991a, 1992b)

Disclosure in elementary schools

During the crucial developmental years of elementary school, children are exposed to a variety of experiential art activities and encouraged to manipulate numerous media. The world of young children is profoundly egocentric, and student artifacts usually reflect this developmental characteristic through the depiction of personal stories.[120] **Students in the elementary grades, therefore, usually participate in episodes of self-disclosure. From the child's perspective, the focus of these self-grounded activities is not the production of artifacts per se but rather a degree of therapeutic, cathartic release obtained through the process of disclosing inner thoughts.** This type of artistic activity is deeply personal even though it occurs within an institutional setting and can be referred to as *private art.* **Elementary school art curricula based upon therapeutic self-disclosure are frequently taught within a multi-disciplinary context, since the traditional** approach of education through art is deeply entrenched at those grade levels. School art programmes that focus upon therapeutic self-disclosure are usually organized as *integrated arts*; they were designed to complement theories of child development and the principles of creative expressionism.

Disclosure in academic secondary schools

Students enroled in art courses in academic secondary schools also disclose personal thoughts; however, unlike elementary children who pursue cathartic release, such students are more frequently focused upon aesthetic form. Art curricula within academic secondary schools usually operate within the framework of aesthetic self-disclosure. They provide studio activities that incorporate both process and product, develop awareness of historical art forms, and foster self- and group-based critiquing skills. They function, therefore, within the modality of *public art*. The roots of contemporary high school curricula focused upon aesthetic self-disclosure can be traced to the accomplishments curricula originally designed for upper-class girls circa 1880. Such programmes reflect the Western academy tradition and can be described as *fine arts*.

Disclosure in vocational secondary schools

Art students enroled in vocational secondary schools are also involved in studio activities that disclose information; however, they are usually not disclosing personal ideas, but iconographic images that can be understood by the public-at-large. Vocational art curricula operate within the framework of utilitarian cultural-disclosure and stress *popular art* activities that result in the production of artifacts intended primarily for industrial or commercial use. Contemporary school programmes based upon utilitarian cultural-disclosure derive their distinctive character from 19th century drawing classes which emphasized mechanical, linear drawing. Such curricula carry on the Western guild tradition and can be categorized as *applied arts*.

It should be understood that the curricular model presented in *Figure 3c: Role of Disclosure within Art Education* was deliberately configured to reflect current pedagogic realities. It is quite possible, however, to envisage patterns of student disclosure beyond those presented in *Figure 3c*. For example, elementary students are quite capable of producing artifacts which demonstrate aesthetic and/or utilitarian qualities, and adults can certainly benefit from episodes of therapeutic self-disclosure. As well, it should be re-emphasized that the matrix presented in *Figure 3c* should be viewed as the foundation for a K-12 art continuum, rather than three discrete curricular strands.

The exercise of judgment in the making of artistic images or in their appreciation depends upon the ability to cope with ambiguity, to experience nuance, and to weigh the tradeoffs among alternative courses of action. These skills not only represent the mind operating in its finest hour but are precisely the skills that characterize our most complex adult life tasks. The problems that perplex us as adults are not those that can be treated by algorithms and verified by proof. School programs that inadvertently teach children there is a correct answer to each important problem they encounter mis-teach children in serious ways. The cultivation of judgment and the ability to be flexibly purposive is best achieved when the tasks and content children encounter in school provide the space for such skills to operate. When the arts are well taught, such skills have an essential place. (p. 67)

Elliot Eisner (1985)
Why art in education and why art education?

In this chapter the practice-based aspects of art pedagogy will be highlighted. It should be understood at the outset, however, that the various attributes listed by Elliot Eisner, those which he asserts afford the arts their fundamental legitimacy within school curricula, will provide the framework for our deliberations.

Two of the key phrases used by Eisner elegantly encapsulate the essence of sound arts pedagogy: *the cultivation of judgement* and *the ability to be flexibly purposive*. While the nurturance of these two abilities can be achieved through student activities centred upon artistic production or aesthetic response, it should be noted that Eisner does not discuss them within the context of arts curricula but within the wider domain of life experiences. Thus, the essential value of arts education in our schools is not the production of artifacts per se, such as murals, monologues, or mazurkas, but the positing of activities that ask students to cope with ambiguity, experience nuance, and weigh alternative courses of action. The arts provide a critical balance to other school subjects that typically stress universal laws, correct responses, and discrete solutions.

Art pedagogy, therefore, is essentially divergent both in purpose and in design; it stands in contrast to the convergent approaches traditionally used within subjects such as science and mathematics. It is certainly possible to teach art through convergent activities, by utilizing teacher-prepared diagrams and worksheets or by emphasizing historical and technical facts, but such strategies do not allow students or teachers to access the existentially rich experiences that art has to offer.

In this chapter, **pedagogic strategies should be viewed as a series of curricular continua spanning kindergarten to grade 12.** Teaching methodology texts often present strategies suitable only for elementary or secondary school learners. In doing so, they fail to provide the bridging techniques crucial for intermediate grades. Perhaps even more damaging, however, is the fact that such texts give the false impression curricula can be planned in isolated blocks or as separate activities. Whether curricula are organized through subject areas such as art and music, or by generic thinking skills such as problem-solving and creativity, activities cannot be implemented without consideration being given to the questions *"What does this lesson build upon?"* and *"What will this lesson contribute to?"*. Education does not begin or end; it is a series of continua that weave "the seamless web of knowledge".[121]

4.1   Preparing for art

Studio as a method of nondirective teaching

Teachers and administrators unfamiliar with art are often perplexed by the dynamics of studio activities. Such educators mistakenly see art classrooms as innately noisy, chaotic, unruly, unfocused, messy, et cetera. At best, they are seen as utterly bewildering and, at worst, simply unprofessional. Usually the root cause of such misconceptions is a lack of understanding of what the term studio means. Studio is not just an artsy term for a classroom; rather, studio refers to a method of nondirective teaching. **Studio is an activity, as well as a place.**

Central to the notion of studio activities is a shift in the *locus of control*, away from the teacher in whom primary control is vested within convergent learning, and towards each student in the class. This shift in locus of control should be maintained consistently, from the early selection of media and subject matter, through to the later assessment of student progress.

Students involved in studio activities are continually confronted with choices that need personal resolution, such as *"Is this line too bold?"*, *"Should a symmetrical design be used within my sculpture?"*, *"Does this pen-and-ink drawing need a coloured wash?"* and so on. Within the operation of a working studio environment, **resolutions to such issues reside primarily within the students**; each will personally decide how to respond.

Sometimes, however, students remain uncertain as to which course of action to take and feel the need to seek out advice. Again, within the context of a working studio environment, such advice is typically sought from fellow students. This process often requires students to leave their own work area and walk around the room, an action rarely necessary in teacher-centred, convergent learning. Students usually walk directly to where a classmate they feel can help them is sitting; in other instances, students may need to observe several peers at work in order to garner a wider perspective. In either situation, **conversations with classmates are a natural part of studio interactions**.

Hence, the origin of the student walking and talking that administrators are so adept at observing through the windows of classroom doors. Such phenomena indicate normalcy within studio activities; surprisingly to some, they signify on-task behaviour. The so-called chaos observed in art classrooms is actually an orderly, complex form of self- and peer instruction.

Teacher roles during studio

Are there no roles for the teacher to play during studio activity? Yes, there are, but they are ones that many educators are unaccustomed to playing:

> The teacher's role fluctuates according to the needs of the students. He plans learning experiences in which the students have to work individually, seeking out knowledge on their own; and he designs other activities where students join with others to carry out a task and where discovery through action is attempted. The teacher is, therefore, not an interpreter, director or controller. Rather, at different times within the same lesson, he can be an advisor, a consultant, a questioner, or a sounding board. Even, at times, he can be a guide. (Courtney, 1980, p. 76)

Teachers are adept at pedagogic roles that place themselves at the apex of instructional activities. They have no trouble in presenting themselves as the repository of important facts, the arbiter between warring factions, or the embodiment of all that is good in public education; but none of those roles fulfil the primary responsibility of teachers during studio activities, which is the nurturing of *artistic disclosure*[122] within individual students.

The nurturing of artistic disclosure requires teachers to develop relationships with students that closely parallel those between parents and their children.[123] The degree of direct intervention by parents in the lives of their children steadily declines as the young people are given opportunities to explore and express their senses of self. Although parents understand that this natural development necessitates a gradual change in their custodial role, they frequently find its reality difficult to accept. The tendency to belittle early attempts at new tasks, to impose adult standards of behaviour, and to resent developing independence are pitfalls that all parents can identify with. The greatest impediment to the healthy development of children, however, is the instinctive parental impulse to shield children from failure by directly intervening in the making of decisions.

Similarly, **the nurturance of artistic disclosure requires a gradual reduction in the degree to which teachers directly intervene during artistic activities.** Sensing the appropriate degree of withdrawal may be difficult at first for teachers with non-arts backgrounds; however, the professional observation of studio dynamics, coupled with experience over time, will help them develop a repertoire of nondirective pedagogic strategies.

In order to feel comfortable with the gradual shift in locus of control from teacher to student, individual **practitioners need to operate within thresholds of professional security.** In *The Dramatic Curriculum*, Richard Courtney cites seven thresholds of pedagogic security[124] originally devised by British drama educator Dorothy Heathcote. Although these thresholds are described in the context of drama within *Figure 4a: Thresholds of Pedagogic Security* they can easily be applied to art; indeed, they can be useful in most areas of educational activity.

Thus far, the process of preparation for studio activities has been discussed in terms of:

- understanding that studio refers to a method of nondirective pedagogy wherein decisions are resolved primarily by each student, secondarily by peers, and lastly by the teacher;
- accepting that the pedagogic locus of control should, as learners mature, gradually shift from teacher to student; and
- acknowledging that practitioners need to feel secure in their roles as teacher through the reflective assessment of seven thresholds of pedagogic security: noise, space, size of group, decision-making, teacher interests, evaluation & standards, and role.

Noise Threshold
Some teachers are discomforted by a greater level of class noise than others. It is better never to become involved in a situation with which one is not comfortable--although noise level is of less importance than noise quality.

Space Threshold
Some prefer to teach with students near to them. Others prefer to teach at a distance. Neither is better or worse than the other--but the teacher should understand the reason for his choice and its consequences.

Size of Group Threshold
Drama activities vary from individual to whole class work. Some teachers are happier with one rather than the other. Initial teachers often start with the individual or pairs, waiting for experience to allow them the comfort of large groups.

Decision-making Threshold
Drama activity involves much decision-making and in varying styles. The secure teacher can employ them all and allow leadership to occur in every type of situation.

Teacher Interests Threshold
It is important that the teacher's own interests do not interfere with the class working. He should remain open to how to begin, suitable themes, and all approaches to dramatic action.

Evaluation and Standards Thresholds
Teachers vary in what they value and, therefore, in what they look for in the students' actions.

Role Threshold
Although the teacher must be in conscious control of the group, the *"I'm telling you"* role should not be used very often. The teacher's role should be varied, from moment to moment, as the drama and the class require.

Figure 4a: Thresholds of Pedagogic Security

(Courtney, 1980)

Trust as the foundation for studio

Underpinning each of these elements is a common foundation that, while implicitly practised by many educators, needs to be explicitly promoted: *trust*. **Successful nondirective pedagogies are wholly dependent upon the establishment and maintenance of trust, both on the part of the teacher and the students involved.**

The key goal of student disclosure during artistic activity is a recurring theme throughout this book. Regardless of what form it takes, disclosure is an innately personal act; it springs from the very core of self. Even for adults, public episodes of disclosure can be deeply unsettling; and, once undertaken, they possess a degree of fragility that seeks immediate acceptance. Failure to secure such acceptance reduces greatly the likelihood that public disclosure will be willingly repeated.

When teachers ask students to disclose personally meaningful information during art classes, they must rely upon a previously fostered atmosphere of trust. In this regard, elementary school teachers have an advantage, in that they usually teach the same students for greater portions of the school day than do secondary teachers. Primary grade teachers, in particular, are in the best position to establish trust due to the innocence of their pupils. The maintenance of such trust is particularly important, although inherently more difficult, for the teachers of adolescent students.

As with most human emotions, **trust needs to operate within a reciprocal arrangement**. Not only do the students need to believe that the teacher will accept whatever they choose to disclose via their work, the teacher also needs to believe that the students will act responsibly with the curricular freedom granted to them. The nondirective pedagogies required for the nurturing of student disclosure demand a level of trust in students that practitioners often find difficult to muster; however, the failure to trust students and the retention of overt control at the teacher's desk suffocate the studio dynamics required for personal disclosure.

4.2   Planning for art

The fundamental structure of art curricula, as charted within *Figure 4b: Curricular Sequence for Art Education*, closely parallels other planning models developed by contemporary curriculum theorists.[125]   It is not possible in this brief section to provide an exhaustive look at curriculum planning; therefore, the following pages will be devoted to the distinguishing aspects of art curricula. For example, since the process of preparing lesson plans for art is essentially the same as for other school subjects, lesson planning will not be highlighted in *Section 4.2*.

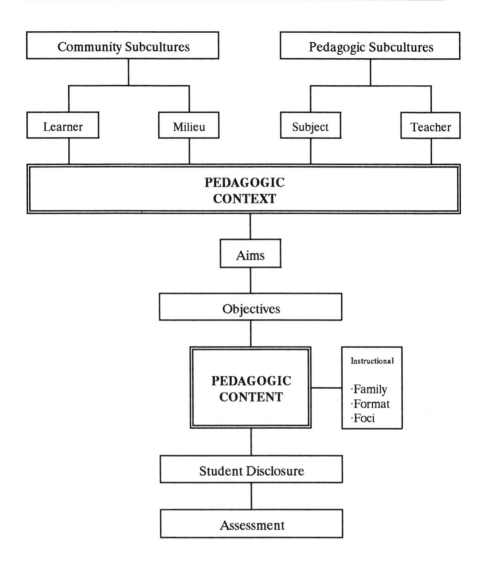

Figure 4b: Curricular Sequence for Art Education

(Clark)

Curriculum commonplaces

Chapter 2 outlined how subject and teacher orientations can produce pedagogic subcultures, and illustrated through documents prepared during the 1980s by the Ontario Ministry of Education how such subcultures could be ignored by planners. Curriculum planners frequently fail to accommodate pedagogic subcultures; they assume that all school subjects are essentially the same and can be taught within a common curricular framework. In the Ontario study, planners focused exclusively upon 13 student-based objectives, statements which determined the curricular parameters for all subject guidelines.[126]

Curricular planning, however, cannot focus exclusively upon the needs of only the students; each of the following factors must be considered concurrently:

teacher characteristics and beliefs;

subject matter, or content;

students needs and characteristics;

teacher's knowledge of principles and techniques;

teaching and learning conditions.[127]

These factors parallel **the *curriculum commonplaces* of learner, milieu, subject and teacher**, developed by Joseph Schwab.[128] Collectively, **they provide the *pedagogic context* with which generalized aims and learner-specific objectives can be derived**. The pedagogic context outlined within *Figure 4b* uses all four Schwabian commonplaces; other current models rely upon similar concepts. For example, Leslie Huling-Austin and W. Robert Houston have developed a framework consisting of four antecedent variables: learner characteristics, teacher characteristics, environmental culture, and instructional conditions.[129] Curiously absent from the Huling-Austin & Houston model is any acknowledgement of the central role played by subject matter, the implications of which are discussed in *Section 2.2: The Reality of Pedagogic Subcultures.*

Instructional families

As discussed in Chapter 1, questions such as *"What kinds of knowledge are the most important?"* and *"How best can knowledge be shared among individuals or groups?"* have sparked debates for centuries, and the inability of educational theorists to provide definitive answers to such fundamental questions continues.

Since 1900, studies within the field of curriculum have produced numerous models of pedagogy, and **the current array of teaching models can be grouped within the four *instructional families*** described in *Figure 4c: Instructional Families.*

Practitioners are thus confronted with a diverse menu of instructional families with which they can implement curricula. Art educators utilize most of these strategies at one time or another, however, **the nurturing of student disclosure is most naturally promoted through the self-grounded *personal family***:

In general, the personal family models of teaching describe learning environments that hope to nurture students rather than to control the sequence of learning. These models are more concerned with long-term learning styles and with developing individual personalities than they are with short-term instructional or content objectives. (Joyce, Weil & Showers, 1991, p. 263)

Certainly, art teachers rarely see students as "self-correcting communication systems", to use the terminology of the behavioural systems family.

The Social Family
Pedagogic strategies within this family include cooperative inquiry, role playing, and case studies. These social models seek to build learning communities and positive school cultures based upon collective energies.

The Information-Processing Family
Approaches within this cluster involve inductive cognition, concept attainment, memory assists, advance organizers, inquiry training, and synectics. These intellectual models seek to help students master information and concepts; collectively, they form the nucleus of curricula based upon thinking skills.

The Personal Family
Pedagogic strategies within this family emphasize nondirective instruction and self-concept enhancement. This cluster focuses upon the perspective of the individual and strives to encourage self-awareness and personal growth.

The Behavioural Systems Family
This cluster focuses upon mastery learning, direct instruction, social learning, self-control management, theory-to-practice, and simulations. These strategies stem from the premise that learners are self-correcting communication systems capable of modifying behaviours in response to performance feedback.

Figure 4c: Instructional Families

(Joyce, Weil & Showers, 1992)

The instructional family, in conjunction with *instructional format* and *instructional foci,* create the *pedagogic content* upon which episodes of student disclosure can be logically structured. *Figure 4b: Curricular Sequence for Art Education,* indicates the interrelationships that exist among these fundamental elements.

Instructional formats

In addition to the selection of an instructional family, the planning of pedagogic content requires an instructional format. In the case of art curricula, **there are two instructional formats to choose from:** *education through art* **or** *education in art.*

The education through art format is most commonly found in elementary school programs where artistic or aesthetic activities are employed as vehicles for the acquisition of generic skills. For example, pictures may be shown as motivational devices prior to a lesson in writing short stories. Still-life drawings may be undertaken in order to develop eye & hand coordination. Murals may be completed by the entire class as a method of fostering acceptable social interactions among students. Although in such cases the emphasis is not upon art per se, valid artistic or aesthetic growth remains achievable, albeit indirectly.

This is the instructional format of preference in elementary schools for three important reasons. First, the manipulation of artistic media facilitates the activity-based learning approaches espoused by educators such as John Dewey and Maria Montessori. Second, media manipulation complements the developmental stage theory of Jean Piaget with its emphasis upon concrete operations. Third, the education through art format accommodates the fact that young children are taught by generalist teachers who often lack any formal art education themselves.

There are, however, some potential dangers associated with the education through art format which need to be scrupulously avoided, such as:

- the absence of curricular activities that focus upon art as a discrete form of knowledge;
- any implicit suggestion that art is of secondary educational value; and
- the mis-teaching of artistic and aesthetic activities by non-specialist educators.

The alternate instructional format, education in art, views art as a separate subject discipline, directly focused upon artistic and/or aesthetic development. Virtually all secondary school art programs are based upon this format, for reasons both historical and practical.[130]   Historically, the arts emerged as secondary school subjects from within the protective custody of previously established curricula: art from mechanical drawing, dance from physical education, drama from English, and music from privately-operated conservatories.   Such disparate points of entry into the curricular mainstream, and at different points in time, made it impossible to develop interdisciplinary or intradisciplinary arts curricula. Practically, the need for subject specialists and their prerequisite performance skills made it unlikely that the arts would, or could, be taught by generalists at the secondary school level.

It must be understood that either of these two instructional formats can be selected when planning elementary or secondary art curricula. The traditional dominance of one in elementary schools and the other in secondary schools, however, is a good example of how curricular structures reflect the realities of pedagogic practice.

The third element of pedagogic content is instructional focus. Art instruction may focus upon *studio, criticism,* **or** *history.* All three instructional foci should contribute to art courses of study, units, and lessons from kindergarten through to grade 12. Each focus should be planned as a learning continuum that stresses learner-appropriate objectives, vocabulary, and activities at each grade level. *Figure 4d: Instructional Foci for Art Education* suggests an instructional menu for each focal area.

Instructional focus: Art studio

The instructional menu for art studio involves three traditional categories: *media, composition,* **and** *theme.* **Media-centred studio curricula contain units of drawing, painting, printmaking, and sculpture**; as well, more contemporary media such as photography, video, and computers[131] are becoming commonplace, even in elementary curricula. There are, however, dangers related to media-centred studio that teachers need to be aware of. One concerns teacher expectations, most notoriously common within art education, that students can master new media without the benefit of *practice* or repetition:

> Visual arts educators are justified in their objections to the type of mindless drill often associated with traditional approaches to content subjects. But there is a middle ground. They could adopt those strategies that have been recognized and employed by exemplary teachers in the larger arts family. Many in music, in drama, and in physical education have demonstrated that practice can provide the ground work and the stimulus for creative thinking. Their students are not asked in each session to begin at zero, but rather to refine, to elaborate, to push back known boundaries, and ultimately to analyze and synthesize. Their students sing songs again and again, strengthen their skills,

ART STUDIO

Media	*Composition*	*Theme*
Drawing	Elements	
Painting	■ Line	
Printmaking	■ Colour	
Sculpture	■ Shape	
Mixed Media	■ Texture	
Photography	■ Value	
Computer		
Video	Principles	
et cetera	■ Balance	
	■ Contrast	
	■ Emphasis	
	■ Movement	
	■ Unity	

ART CRITICISM

■ Description
■ Analysis
■ Interpretation
■ Judgement

ART HISTORY

Chronological
Monumental
Biographical
Experiential

Figure 4d: Instructional Foci for Art Education

(Clark)

and develop repertoires that can serve as spring-boards for creative self-expression. (Fast, 1989, p. 52)

An additional cautionary note involves the potential for an over-emphasis upon studio activities, at the expense of art criticism and art history:

> Though schools have not typically provided instruction
> which reflects art's value and complexity,...learning art
> requires more than looking at or trying to produce
> artworks. One needs to understand the historical and
> cultural contributions of art and how to analyze and
> interpret artistic compositions. Research found, however,
> that even schools concerned with teaching art tend to
> emphasize art-making activities to the exclusion of critical
> and art historical study. (Getty, 1985, p. 3)

Studio activities may also be structured around the elements and principles of composition, or design. Although actual lists of elements and principles often vary from text to text, these are most frequently cited:

Elements of Composition	*Principles of Composition*
colour	balance
line	contrast
shape	emphasis
texture	movement
value	unity

Compositional elements are the building blocks, so to speak, with which messages disclosed by students are given physical form. In the case of nonobjective works, they are applied in their purest forms, devoid of any representational depiction. The elements of composition should be emphasized during lessons at the elementary school level; compositional principles should be introduced to students during senior elementary grades. The principles are achieved by the selective usage of one or more compositional elements. For example, the principle of balance could be achieved by lines, shapes, or colours, et cetera of equal visual importance.

The traditional application of compositional elements and principles in the analysis of art objects is known as *formalism*. Formalism is the artistic equivalent of grammar, and its utilization during picture analysis is akin to parsing sentences. The teaching of visual scanning skills based upon formalist rules is as contentious within art education as the teaching of grammar is within language arts. This book, however, is premised upon the belief that sound art curricula encompass pedagogic strategies that address both left- and right-brain processes of cognition, and the broad diversity of learning styles discussed within *Section 4.3: Monitoring Art*. Thus, there is a place for formalism within art education, as long as it is balanced by other instructional activities that develop intuitively-based analytic skills.

The third method of organizing studio activities involves the use of a theme, or subject matter. This approach to studio planning is easily the most popular, especially among generalist practitioners who often know little about media or composition. Thematic planning can be employed to integrate, or relate, art experiences with the broader school curricula. Themes can also bridge school activities with events occurring within the local community. In short, thematic planning can be very helpful in making art an integral part of each student's educational experience. There are, however, cautionary elements to this instructional focus:

- Thematic approaches can often result in repetitious lessons directed towards superficial art activities, such as classroom decoration or holiday celebrations.[132]
- Teacher-assigned themes often reduce student motivation by keeping "ownership" for the activity at the teacher's desk.
- Teacher-assigned themes run the risk of being inappropriate for students if too juvenile, too sophisticated, too vague, or too well-defined.
- Thematic approaches can often be used to cover an avoidance of professional instruction in art media or art history.

The biggest problem with the thematic model, however, is its incompatibility with the fundamental art goal of personally relevant student disclosure. These weaknesses can be greatly reduced by allowing the students to select their own subject content and organizing the instruction around media or composition. Teachers need to be prepared, however, for some of the consequences of thematic choice:

- Student-selected themes are often overtly gender specific and, frequently, "politically incorrect".
- Adolescent themes often include depictions of violent or sexual activities.
- Student-selected themes frequently require technical skills beyond the capability of the students to perform.
- Individualized themes increase the complexity of normative assessment.
- Student-selected themes often reveal discordant family relationships or personal social conflicts.

These issues are particularly problematic for practitioners who are unwilling or unable to cope with such pedagogic realities, or who teach emotionally-challenged students.

Instructional focus: Art criticism

Pedagogic content also involves a focus upon art criticism. This focus is the least common, especially within elementary art curricula, largely due to generalist teachers' unfamiliarity with the field. The traditional dominance of studio activities within art education has, since the 1980s, been widely criticized by proponents of movements such as discipline-based art education. Gradually, performance activities are being balanced by lessons focused upon art appreciation; knowledge *about* art has become as important as knowledge *in* art. Hence, the need for criticism within art pedagogic content:

> Why do we enjoy talking about art? Because it is one of the best ways to communicate our feelings without embarrassment. That may be why few people can resist the impulse to deliver critical judgments: we want others to *know* us in a special way. But the great critics have more than a desire to talk; they have an unusually rich and varied capacity for aesthetic pleasure. By disclosing their discoveries they enlarge our capacities for understanding and delight. In this sense, art criticism is like teaching; it is the communication of ideas about art--and often about life, the soil in which art is nourished. (Feldman, 1987, p. 454)

This text has consistently stressed the central goal of student disclosure within art education. Disclosure-based activities are primarily structured to help students acquire a personal knowledge of self but, as Edmund Burke Feldman points out, "by disclosing their discoveries", students secondarily help "others to *know* [them] in a special way."

We respond to artistic disclosures every time we listen to music on the car radio or watch movies on the television set. In such informal situations we are able to respond critically without much hesitation. Within more formal settings such as art galleries or concert halls, however, it is often much more difficult "to communicate our feelings without embarrassment."

Our desire to respond does not diminish, but the complexities of content and context overwhelm our critical assessment skills.

Laura Chapman has devised a logical, practical, and sequential framework for art criticism, which is described within *Figure 4e: Instructional Sequence for Art Criticism.* Chapman's model consists of four major steps: describing what you see, analyzing relations, interpreting meanings, and judging.

> Art criticism is more than saying "I like it" or "I don't like
> it." It is a step-by-step process of logical thinking. Similar
> steps are used by scientists, lawyers, and others who present
> ideas clearly. (Chapman, 1992, p. 67)

Chapman's assertion that artistic response is simply a "process of logical
thinking", not unlike the cognitive processes used within scientific inquiry,
parallels Sharon Bailin's[133] claim that artistic performance operates
primarily through logical cognition.

Description: What do you see?

This first step involves an objective, factual description of
the work using topics such as: artform, media, and
condition; dimensions; subject matter; sensory qualities; and
technical qualities.

Analysis: How is the work planned?

The formal qualities of the work are analyzed in order to
discover relationships such as: balance; rhythm and
movement; proportions; emphasis; pattern; unity and
variety; and relationships in subject matter.

Interpretation: What are the expressive qualities?

The expressive qualities of the work are interpreted though:
expressive language; analogies; intrapersonal responses; and
the relating of subject matter to life experiences.

Judgement: How artistically valuable is the work?

This process involves: identifying the kind of work being
judged; stating your purpose for judging the work;
identifying the criteria or standards being used; citing
evidence or reasons; and stating your conclusions.

Figure 4e: Instructional Sequence for Art Criticism

(Chapman, 1992)

Feldman (1989) has developed a similar four-step approach to art criticism which also relies heavily upon logical cognition: "we encourage students to argue logically from visual evidence, to form hypotheses, to reason deductively and inductively, to build an art vocabulary, and to translate from the visual to the verbal" (p. 10).

Instructional focus: Art history

The third focus upon which art pedagogic content may be structured is art history. Art history is an essential part of any comprehensive art curriculum because *antecedent traditions* play key roles within the two instructional foci previously discussed, art studio and art criticism:

> Artists are continually influenced by the events of the world around them as well as by what other artists are doing. They are also greatly influenced by what artists have previously done, and thus they, in turn, will influence those yet to come. Children should personally experience and come to appreciate that there are certain basic vocabularies associated with making meaning through images, sounds, movements, and words.[134] In this way, children will learn to *read* works of art in each of the arts disciplines, thereby learning forms of cultural literacy. (Irwin, 1992a, p. 26)

Rita Irwin's studio-grounded contention that contemporary artists are "greatly influenced by what artists have previously done", parallels Sharon Bailin's philosophic assertion that acts of originality are rooted within antecedent traditions that can be identified in all works of art.[135] Originality is not an absolute quality that artifacts either do or do not exhibit; rather, works of art lie somewhere along a continuum of creativity which ranges from minor variations-on-a-theme to major breaks with tradition. Thus, art history and studio are inherently intertwined; studio activities are contextualized by historical traditions. As well, antecedent traditions provide a measure with which contemporary works can be valued and evaluated.

Art history can be planned within any one of four curricular approaches. The most common method is *chronological,* whereby developments are surveyed, beginning with prehistorical exemplars and proceeding through to contemporary works. The chronological approach is typically a university and secondary school model; it is not very appropriate for young children whose conceptual awareness of time is largely undeveloped:[136]

> In the early childhood classroom, art history should not be addressed in a chronological way. Rather, thematic groupings of reproductions or original works of art will spark enthusiasm for specific subject matter. For example, viewing a variety of portraits from different time periods

would introduce students to the idea that some artists are concerned with recording imagination, or showing emotions through distorted colours. At the child's level, this kind of interaction with works of art will teach them that all kinds of art are valued in our society. (Irwin, 1992a, p. 26)

In this passage, Irwin has described the second most common approach to art history, *monumental,* **in which students interact with works of art.** Works are usually preselected on the basis of thematic content or studio technique.

Art history may also be taught using a *biographical* **model in which students focus upon the artists responsible for various works.** An advantage to this approach is that artistic activities can be humanized and given an everyday context that students can relate to. Insights into how artists in the past dealt with internal, creative processes and external, sociological pressures help the student artists of today cope with their own creative dilemmas. Feldman's 1982 text, *The Artist,* was based upon this biographical approach, and used the following chapter headings: the shaman, child artists and naive artists, peasant and folk artists, the classical artisan, the medieval guildsman, the renaissance genius, the revolutionary artist, the bohemian artist, the illustrator, the industrial designer, the gallery idol, and the hyphenated artist.

Art history may also be approached *experientially.* Annie Smith has developed several strategies for helping students experience the creative and/or aesthetic essences of major historical works.[137] Experiential strategies require students to explore symbiotic relationships that exist between art studio and art history. The following passage illustrates the logical progression of inquiry that this form of creative interplay can take:

> What was the tradition of place mats anyway, and when did they start? The fifteenth century Flemish portrayals of the Last Supper had tablecloths in them. Did the T'sang Dynasty have tablecloths? Table cloths? Clothes for the table? Different styles of tables from different eras would naturally require different styles of dress. And would we not dress the legs? Would Rococo table legs wear panty hose, and would a Charles Rene Mackintosh bed stand have plaid socks? And do we shoe the little table feet? For that we must know something about the history of shoes. Ah, another art history project, and we are off and running up all sorts of historical avenues. (Smith, 1992a, pp. 10-11)

Clearly, such experiential approaches provide easy linkages between studio and art history; as well, experiential strategies can facilitate learning among the collective arts. Critics of this approach, however, suggest that such activities have the potential to trivialize art history by distorting the cultural value and the original purpose behind historical works. The main deterrent to experiential art history, though, is the need for students and teachers to be cognisant of historically significant styles and artists.

Whether one teaches art history using a chronological, monumental, biographical, or experiential approach, **the selection of significant works must be undertaken with great care.** The limited amount of instructional time available for art history within most curricula considerably reduces the number of works that can be introduced to learners. Most texts and reproductions available to teachers reflect histories that are profoundly male and Eurocentric;[138] such biased exemplars are especially problematic for art instruction within multicultural settings. The selection of artifacts that adequately represent local, national, and global achievements in art, can be further complicated by political pressures focused upon nationalistic and patriotic agendas.

The selection of appropriate exemplars might, at this point, seem to be an overwhelming task. Generalist educators should be aware, however, that even art specialists fall prey to criticism in this task. In the following passage, Karen Hamblen (1986) outlines the dilemma facing art historians in our contemporary, multicultural society:

> Art literature is rife with intimations that art speaks a universal language, that it transcends the exigencies of time and space, and that it binds us together in our common humanity (Mukerjee, 1954; Read, 1965). Conversely, one also finds, although perhaps less commonly, criticism of broad claims for aesthetic universalism (Chalmers, 1978; Kamp, 1973). These latter critics believe that the assumption that art cuts across cultural boundaries has obscured the rich diversity of artistic meanings and has often resulted in the ignoring of art forms and life styles outside major Western cultures. To be fully appreciated, art needs to be understood within the context of its originating culture's values, symbolism, and functions. (p. 69)

The resolution of this dilemma certainly lies beyond the scope of this text. However, opportunities for self-grounded student disclosures, especially those within culturally diverse instructional settings, reduce the burden of exemplar selection. In such instances, cultural enrichment can be naturally obtained by observing and discussing works produced by minority students, which frequently display non-Western treatments of picture plane, use of colour, et cetera.

Stages of child art development

Effective instructional planning also requires practitioners to be aware of the *developmental stages* that children go through in art. There are several developmental models currently popular in the literature that describe the process of art maturation,[18] but despite the disparate number of stages each model suggests, the sequence of development each model describes is very similar:

> The first stage is one at which children manipulate materials, initially in an exploratory, random fashion. Later in this stage the manipulation becomes increasingly organized until the children give a title to the marks they make. During the next stage, the children develop a series of distinct symbols that stand for objects in their experience. These symbols are eventually related to an environment within the drawing. Finally comes a preadolescent stage, at which the children become critical of their work and express themselves in a more self-conscious manner. (Gaitskell, Hurwitz & Day, 1982, p. 144)

The model selected for this chapter was originally developed by Ontario art theorist Charles Dudley Gaitskell in his classic book, *Children and Their Art*. Now in its fourth printing, the text currently contains material supplied by two co-authors from the United States, Al Hurwitz, and Michael Day.

Developmental Stage	*Grades in School*
Manipulative Stage	Early Childhood
Symbol-Making Stage	Grades 1-4
Preadolescent Stage	Grades 5-8

Figure 4f: Developmental Model for Art Education

(Gaitskell, Hurwitz & Day, 1982)

Manipulative Stage   *Early Childhood*

The first stage of child art development is the manipulative stage, or *scribbling*. Young children are fascinated to discover that they can control the production of images through deliberate motor action. Although their choice of media and picture grounds may leave a lot to be desired, it is important that parents not discourage young children at this stage. The scribbled images are often repeated many times; the resultant kinaesthetic motion helps to develop gross motor control and is emotionally soothing. Scribbling begins with *random marking*, develops into *controlled manipulation*, and eventually results in the production of shapes that receive *names*, or titles. Individual children will progress through these steps at their own pace, however, by the end of the manipulative stage most child art shares several characteristics:

- The work of art is primarily instrumental in nature; in other words, it is an adjunct of another thought process rather than an end in itself. This does not preclude, however, drawing as a self-rewarding act.
- Early drawings are general rather than specific; that is, they deal with dominant impressions as opposed to differentiation. (Noses may be more significant than the roundness of the head.)
- Each stage of development is usually accompanied by a period of retrenchment, often regression, during which the schemas are repeated in a seemingly mechanistic way. (Gaitskell, Hurwitz & Day, 1982, p. 149)

Symbol-Making Stage   *Grades 1-4*
                        6-9

After children begin to assign names to objects that they produce, *symbolic shapes* representing common pictorial elements, such as "Mommy" and "our house", start to appear. At first, the symbols are undifferentiated; a rudimentary shape developed to represent "our dog" may also be used to represent "your cat". In time, more details are added, and differences between similar shapes, such those between "Mommy" and "Aunt Mary", are noted.

It is at this stage that stereotypical elements begin to emerge; for example, landscapes often involve:

- using the bottom of the page to represent the ground.
- creating a horizon line where the ground meets the sky.
- locating the sun in either top corner.
- filling the sky with white clouds and black birds.
- showing smoke coming from chimneys, and so on.

Given the freedom to choose, children usually want to tell stories about themselves and their immediate world. They "see" such stories clearly in their minds; **children draw and paint from *memory*, as opposed to drawing and painting from *vision*, as most adults do.** Once this vital difference is understood, many of the following characteristics of child art can be appreciated as the ingenious solutions they actually are, rather than as mistakes that need to be corrected.

When children begin to depict stories that stem from memory, the physical limitations imposed by flat, rectangular sheets of paper demand technical solutions to problems of time and space. In each instance, their pictorial solutions spring from the multiple images that they "see" in their mind's eye:

- When a story involves more than one physical vantage point, *multiple-view drawings* are used. This approach often results in two opposite sides of the same building being depicted simultaneously, for example.

- Sometimes a story can take place inside and outside; in such instances, *x-ray drawings* are produced. Typically, x-ray drawings reveal cut-away sections of buildings, vehicles, et cetera, and occasionally even objects beneath the ground.

- It is not uncommon to find objects repeated within a single picture; such works are called *serial drawings* and they involve stories which occur over a period of time. Adults use a sheet of paper to show what they can see at a glance, and since objects cannot occupy different spaces at the same time, serial drawings are often hard for adults to accept. Adults resolve this problem by dividing the paper into individual blocks, each representing separate "moments in time", a device commonly used in cartoon strips.

- The reliance upon memory in this stage of art development also reveals itself in the absence of objects or viewpoints that children are unfamiliar with, and the non-depiction of objects that are extraneous to the story.

Preadolescent Stage   *Grades 5-8*
9-13

As children approach adolescence they become increasingly self-conscious and concerned about peer acceptance. These two social factors are especially problematic in classes where they are asked to "perform" in front of other students, such as art:

- Students become overly critical of their abilities and easily frustrated by their inability to master technical problems, such as linear perspective or figure drawing.

- Projects are frequently never finished unless they have to be "handed in" for assessment.

- Artifacts produced at this stage are typically small in scale, excessively detailed, and rigidly executed.
- Students are often unwilling to see their work displayed, and are prone to destroying their finished work.
- Boys and girls prefer to work in groups of their own gender and usually select gender-related subject matter.

Teachers need to acknowledge the root causes of these social regressions and employ pedagogic strategies that address such problems directly. First, teachers should appreciate the need students in these grades have for being treated as young adults. Any continued reliance upon juvenile subject matter, materials, or production techniques increases the likelihood of rebellious behaviour during art. Second, art teachers must be prepared to help students produce "adult" work, which usually means realistic representation. The students no longer rely on remembered images and have come to realize that adults do not use multiple-view, x-ray, or serial elements in their artwork. Thus, in this stage of art development, teachers need to provide students with direct art instruction - a real challenge for generalist practitioners:

> Children want to know how to handle overlap, size, and placement relationships, and convergence of lines for representing space and depth in their drawings and paintings. They are receptive to instruction in shading and proportion in drawing. They are interested in the technical aspects of painting, colour mixing, composition, and so on. They are ready to learn about what artists of the past have created and what contemporary artists are doing and why.
> (Gaitskell, Hurwitz & Day, 1982, p. 168)

In spite of such pedagogic demands, teaching art in senior elementary grades can be a fulfilling experience if the social and artistic needs of preadolescent students are professionally addressed.

4.3   Monitoring art

Art education, with its focus upon student disclosure, is most naturally conducted within the self-grounded, nondirective personal family cluster of pedagogic strategies:

> The nondirective teaching model focuses on *facilitating* learning. The primary goal of nondirective teaching is to assist students in attaining greater personal integration, effectiveness, and realistic self-appraisal. A related goal is to create a learning environment conducive to the process

of stimulating, examining, and evaluating new perceptions.
(Joyce, Weil & Showers, 1992, p. 264)

In *Section 4.1: Preparing for Art*, the need for teachers to develop a repertoire of nondirective pedagogic strategies was stressed, and **the necessity of gradually shifting the locus of control from teacher to student was seen as fundamental.** The teacher's role is transformed from that of decision-maker to facilitator, and a partnership is developed between student and teacher.[140]

Teachers as parents

This partnership was likened to the relationships that exist between parents and their children. Indeed, the term *pedagogy* was originally developed in ancient Greece to describe just such a relationship: *paidos* (child) + *agein* (to lead). Broadly speaking, pedagogy refers to those activities planned by an adult to cultivate a child's "positive being and becoming".[141]

This parent/child foundation gives rise to several basic qualities that typify good pedagogy:

a sense of vocation, love of and caring for children, a deep sense of responsibility, moral intuitiveness, self-critical openness, thoughtful maturity, tactful sensitivity toward the child's subjectivity, an interpretive intelligence, a pedagogic understanding of the child's needs, improvisational resoluteness in dealing with young people, a passion for knowing and learning the mysteries of the world, the moral fibre to stand up for something, a certain understanding of the world, active hope in the face of prevailing crises, and, not the least, humour and vitality. (Van Manen, 1991, p. 8)

Max van Manen's description of pedagogy may seem overwhelming, but its essence can be captured within the simple concept of *pedagogic thoughtfulness*,[142] a nondirective approach which offers several self-grounded instructional strategies that can nurture student disclosure:

Van Manen uses four words that I would like to explore to help us locate pedagogy - tone, tact, thoughtfulness, and hope. These are not words that one often hears in school staff rooms (at least not often enough). As pedagogues, says Van Manen, we need to strike the right tone with children. To find the right pitch, to be in tune, we must be tactful. Tact is a particular sensitivity and attunement to situations. Pedagogical tact is having a sensitivity to what is best for each child, for each learner, and having a sense of his or her life and his or her deep pre-occupations. (Pearse, 1992a, p. 62)

Van Manen's approach argues that neither educational theories nor instructional models can fully prepare teachers for *curricular moments*,[143] those times in which teachers interact directly with their students. Van Manen believes that pedagogy is conditioned by love, care, hope, and responsibility for children and, further, he suggests that pedagogic understanding is best achieved through sensitive listening and observing. When dealing directly with students, teachers should employ *pedagogic tact*, a subjective insight which Van Manen defines as "the practice of being oriented to others." Although pedagogic tact cannot be planned in advance of curricular moments, it manifests itself in: holding back, being open to the student's experience, being attuned to subjectivity, influencing students subtly, displaying situational confidence, and being able to improvise when the need arises. Pedagogic tact operates though speech, silence, eye contact, gesture, atmosphere, and by example.

Thus, **the key to monitoring student activity and encouraging artistic expression is trusting students and treating them with consideration and respect**. Clearly, one does not have to be an art specialist to do that; creating a nondirective atmosphere in which artistic disclosure is encouraged can be achieved by every competent teacher. The nondirective atmosphere has four qualities.[144] First, the classroom teacher displays genuine interest in and acceptance of the student as a unique person. Second, a nonjudgemental tone is established. Third, the student is encouraged to verbalize personal viewpoints. And fourth, student-teacher discussions or interviews are non-coercive.

The most common problem that teachers have with nondirective strategies is their tendency to intervene directly when students hesitate to begin work, work too slowly, or ask for assistance:

> It is often terribly trying for an adult to hold back when the child does not seem to know how to do something, when the young person does something wrong at first, or when the student does something so agonizingly slowly. The adult becomes exasperated and is inclined to intervene, to "help", when the child should or may want to deal with the situation himself or herself. Or the adult offers to do it for the child ("here, let me tie your shoelaces!") when the child really needs to figure it out, to learn and to practice.
>
> A tactful understanding of when to hold back, when to pass over things, when to wait, when "not to notice" something, when to step back, rather than to intervene, draw the attention, or interrupt, is a gift to the child's personal development. (Van Manen, 1991, p. 151)

Nondirective instructional strategies do not simply involve holding back and avoiding teacher interventions. Such passive approaches succeed only when they operate within the framework of a comprehensive pedagogy that actively responds to the learning needs of diverse student populations.

Responding to diverse learning styles

Bernice McCarthy (1981) believes that effective curricula actively respond to four fundamental pedagogic questions:
"Why should I learn this material?"
"What material do I need to learn?"
"How does this material work?"
"What can this material become?".

The pedagogic need to answer *"Why?"*, *"What?"*, *"How?"*, and *"What if?"* stems from McCarthy's research into how individuals learn. McCarthy believes that learning begins with perception, which can involve either active, sensory intuition or abstract, intellectual reason. In other words, we can perceive information by sensing/feeling, or by thinking. Perception is followed by processing, which can involve either active experimentation or reflective observation; we can process information by doing, or by watching.

McCarthy uses these two polarized phenomena to construct the *4MAT System*, a learning model with four quadrants. Each quadrant addresses one of the four pedagogic questions and represents a specific learning style. **It is important to understand that for each learning style there is a corresponding teaching style**. The instructional cycle devised by McCarthy requires educators to develop a repertoire of four teaching styles, each of which can be approached using nondirective strategies.

When teachers encounter students who are not constructively engaged in the assigned activity, it is likely that at least one of McCarthy's four pedagogic questions has not been sufficiently answered. Sometimes students fail to see the purpose of the assignment. Answers to *"Why?"* are most readily accepted by students when the assigned activity is explained in such a way that the relevance to their personal, lived experiences is clear.

Generalist practitioners' unfamiliarity with art education often results in minimal amounts of direct instruction or skill demonstration. Incomplete answers to *"What?"* can often be the root cause of student frustration and off-task behaviours. The prevalence of nondirective pedagogic strategies in art education is no excuse for nonexistent content or weak skills. Encouraging creativity requires more than a smile as crayons are given out.

Responding to the pedagogic question *"How?"* is typically an area of strength for art educators, however, behaviour-related problems can develop if too much emphasis is placed upon studio production or performance. In elementary grades, where it is especially important to avoid overt peer competition, cooperative group activities are highly recommended. The need for practice and repetition has been traditionally under stressed in art curricula (Fast, 1989).

Quadrant 1   **The Innovative Learner: "Why?"**
Teaching Style: Discussion

These students learn most readily by perceiving information concretely and processing it reflectively. They absorb reality by listening and sharing ideas. They seek meaning by being personally involved in the lesson.

Quadrant 2   **The Analytic Learner: "What?"**
Teaching Style: Informational

These students learn most easily by perceiving information abstractly and processing it reflectively. They form reality by thinking through ideas.   They seek facts by asking experts what they think.

Quadrant 3   **The Common Sense Learner: "How?"**
Teaching Style: Facilitating

These students learn most readily by perceiving information abstractly and processing it actively. They edit reality by testing theories in ways that seem sensible to them. They seek usability by knowing how things work.

Quadrant 4   **The Dynamic Learner: "What if?"**
Teaching Style: Self-Discovery

These students learn most easily by perceiving information concretely and processing it actively. They enrich reality by self-discovery and trial-by-error.   They seek hidden possibilities by knowing what can be done with things.

Figure 4g: Learning and Teaching Styles

(McCarthy, 1981)

Responding to the pedagogic question *"What if?"* ought to be another area of strength for art education, due to its emphasis upon creativity. As with the question "Why?", answers to "What if?" are ideally suited to activities that link school activities to students' lived experiences in the community. Although the extension of art assignments into other areas of student growth should be part of all students' art curricula, the fascination of hidden possibilities is especially alluring to gifted learners who often require wider pedagogic freedom and greater academic challenge. The failure to provide such opportunities to the art gifted can result in off-task behaviours from "good" students.[145]

Educational venues typically accessed only as enrichment vehicles, such as museums, galleries, and performance centres, need to be seen as integral elements within basic art curricula:

> Many school-based educators think and act as if schools exclusively, or almost so, are capable of providing educational regeneration to make learning both responsive to society and fully satisfying for the individual. History suggests that the national reports that have called for educational reform in the 80's will probably meet the same fate as their predecessors of the last seventy-five years. For the most part they are insular about schools and neglect the possibilities suggested by a richer understanding of non-school educational environments. This requires an open mind about where learning can best be accomplished and to the alternative forms of pedagogy and use of a variety of media and technology associated with learning in non-school settings. In other words, we must put aside our concerns with territoriality to see schooling and education in a fresh light. (Weiss, 1992, p. 1)

Motivating reluctant learners

Not all students enjoy art.

In fact, some students are so frightened at the prospect of having to *perform* in art class that they deliberately misbehave in order to be sent out of the room. Such individuals prefer the certainty of detention over the chance of humiliation.

This is a topic that books on art education rarely address. Proponents of *developmentalism*[146] emphasize the universality of children's innate desire to express themselves through the direct manipulation of concrete materials, and art texts are filled with photographs of happy, on-task learners. But every teacher knows that **not all students can summon the courage to create**.

There may be many reasons why some learners are reluctant to "get started" on their art projects, but three possibilities come most readily to mind: **lack of trust, lack of self-esteem,** and **lack of adequate, direct instruction.** Each of these deficiencies seems to concurrently become most apparent, and most problematic, during senior elementary grades; indeed, not all teachers can summon the courage to teach art in those grades. The solution, of course, is to address the learning deficit that lies at the root of the problem: **instill trust, build self-esteem,** and **provide adequate instruction.** But these are long-term strategies that do not help teachers prod reluctant learners into "getting started" *right now*.

Teachers need to resist turning to short-term strategies, such as showing reluctant students *sample solutions*, or "helping them get started" by suggesting possible themes or doing part of the assignment. Teachers who resort to such methods often claim that "*my students can't get started without a sample in front of them*", and so on. Such claims are undoubtedly true, but only because they are self-fulfilling prophecies. **Although well-intentioned, motivational shortcuts actually increase student reluctance by reinforcing feelings of performance inadequacy.** They send the message, "*You're right, you can't do this work, and because I agree that you can't do this work on your own, I'd rather just do it for you than to try and teach you anything new.*"

Well then, how can art teachers get reluctant learners "going" without reinforcing feelings of performance inadequacy? The solution is to draw upon experiences, backgrounds, and skills that the students already possess. Start building confidence by working with whatever the students bring to the task at hand. Perhaps they have already worked with clay, maybe they live on a farm, or perhaps they know a lot about geometry. **Take whatever the students already know and use it to temporarily displace the unfamiliar task that is causing the performance anxiety.** If the media can be substituted with clay, then clay it is. If the subject matter can be changed to a farm scene, then go for it. If the style can be converted to cubism, then we're off and running.

Art curricula that are comprehensive in scope help ensure that students experience personal success frequently during the school year. Such personal successes provide students with the confidence needed to surmount performance anxieties presented by unfamiliar tasks.

4.4   Assessing art

Common excuses for avoiding art assessment

Perhaps the most contentious element of art education, especially for generalist practitioners, is the assessment of student progress.

Altogether too many adults can recall in vivid detail times when, as children, they were publicly humiliated by insensitive arts teachers. Perhaps their paintings were held up in front of classmates as examples of what not to do; or maybe they were forced to sing a solo piece that was beyond their vocal range; alternatively, they might recall having tried out for a part in the school musical and being assigned the part of a tree. Such performance disasters often result in solemn pledges never to subject their own students to such humiliating experiences. Unfortunately, however, such pledges frequently translate into a wholesale aversion to any form of art assessment whatsoever.

Some educators sidestep student assessment by stressing the subjective nature of artistic expression: *"How can I evaluate somebody else's self-expression?"*. Well, teachers can't, at least not by themselves. **They need to involve their students by activating each learner's internal locus of evaluation:** [147]

> In a creative learning environment, the internal locus of evaluation should rest with the learner. The value of one's creation should be determined by one's own reaction to and appraisal of the creation. In other words, it feels right when one is satisfied with the result knowing that we have approached the project in an authentic way. The learner should be allowed to make mistakes and to learn from these mistakes. This does not mean the mistakes should be ignored but rather used as stepping stones to further problem solving. (Irwin, 1992a, p. 31)

Another altogether too common way of avoiding the assessment of artistic activities is the assignment of teacher-prepared and "student proof" projects. Such curricula result in predictable, often identical artifacts that reduce the need for individualized assessments. Unfortunately, however, they also reduce the degree of artistic disclosure to the point that the assignments become little more than busywork, mere curricular mirages with the appearance of creativity.

Other teachers avoid art assessment by claiming that they are stressing process rather than product, implying that process cannot be validly assessed on its own. The implication is, of course, simply not true. Process-based art activities can be assessed formatively by teachers through clinical observation, anecdotal reporting, or objective-specific checklists. As well, process-based activities can be formatively assessed by students through personal studio journals or in-progress documentation for information files. [148] Such strategies may be accompanied by student interviews or conferences held during various stages of the studio activity.

It should be pointed out, however, that sound art curricula rarely separate process from product. How good can a process be if it does not beg for physical manifestation? Not much. How frequently can good products result merely by chance? Not often. In art, good processes lead to good products and good products result from good processes.

It is true that some elements of art curricula do not lend themselves to assessment. **Experiential activities, such as going to an artist's studio or an art gallery, are frequently spoiled by subsequent classroom assignments.** Such outings are planned to foster positive attitudes toward art and encourage patronage in later life. Assignments greatly reduce the attainment of such goals and often produce the opposite of the results intended.

The biggest enemy that educators face is time. There simply is not enough time to act upon all of the expectations that the public has for the educational system. **Given the crowded state of contemporary school timetables, teachers cannot afford to waste time on unimportant activities.** Once the decision has been taken to include art as part of a comprehensive curriculum, it is the professional responsibility of all practitioners to assess student progress in art and to relay such assessments to students and parents. If, at the conclusion of an art activity, teachers cannot think of anything to report, or, if the non-attainment of the lesson's objectives is of no consequence, it would appear that the students' time has simply been wasted. When students are required to participate in the curriculum, they deserve a response from their teachers and peers, as well as an opportunity to offer a self-assessment of their achievements.

The assessment of student progress ought to be a positive event; surely each student has grown, at least to some degree, as a result of the activities undertaken. Teachers need to realize that students want to share this growth with peers and celebrate what they have accomplished. This is especially true for art activities, since the students discover and disclose a bit about themselves within each studio assignment. Teachers also need to appreciate that assessment strategies are part of the pedagogic cycle. The assessment of student progress not only provides an opportunity for a review of the lesson's original objectives, it also acts as an introduction to future educational activities.

The best time for student learning is not during introductory lessons, but during assessment activities. Teachers often ask their students "*Are there any questions?*" at the conclusion of introductory lessons; if the lessons were competently taught, few questions arise. Students do, however, have valuable comments to offer at the completion of assignments, when they have personally experienced the growth offered by the activities. Unfortunately, however, teachers tend to rush on to the next lesson and neglect to garner student comments when they are most easily elicited and most readily utilized.

The avoidance of student assessment is not restricted to art education. Most people associate assessment with evaluation and evaluation, in turn, with negative criticism. **We need to re-focus assessment processes so that they celebrate accomplishments rather than expose deficiencies.** When devising assessment plans, teachers should seek ways of finding out what students know or what students can do, not what they don't know or can't do. At first, this might seem to be mere semantic play, but it is not. Do students begin with a failing grade and work towards passing, or do they begin from a position of teacher confidence? Can they achieve 100%, or are there factors that keep marks between 40 and 80%? Are the questions worded so that students can demonstrate personally relevant competencies, or are they designed to test for teacher-selected emphases?

Appropriate strategies for art assessment

Art assessment strategies seek to respond to many of the basic evaluative needs shared by other school subjects:

- the need to regard evaluation as a positive component of the student's learning experience;

- the need to relate evaluation activities to the student's level of development;

- the need to use only evaluation activities appropriate to each particular grade, division or subject;

- the need to recognize and address the relationship between stated objective, learning activities and evaluation activities;

- the need to develop evaluation practices which support learning-as-process as well as learning-as-product;

- the need to modify evaluation procedures for exceptional students and to differentiate evaluation for students at different levels of ability;

- the need to continually re-examine evaluation practices; and to be open to changing them should it prove necessary; and

- the need to determine whether or not we are truly evaluating what we *think* we are evaluating.
  (Board of Education for the City of Etobicoke, 1987, p. xiv)

Although art assessment strategies address evaluative needs that are common to other subject areas, **the indirect pedagogic foundation of art education suggests that traditional evaluative approaches, those developed for objective direct instruction, are often inappropriate.** Traditional evaluative approaches reflect *the positivist paradigm,* "a mechanistic view of the world that consists of competencies, checklists, and tiny behaviours that can be assessed".[149]   Consider, for example, the following *performance criteria* prepared by curriculum positivist David Pratt (1980) as a response to the apparently simple, single learning objective, *"The driver will be able to parallel park"*:

> The driver will park the automobile in which he or she expects to take the official driving test between two cars in a space 1-1/2 times the length of the car driven. The driver will stop with the inside wheels within twenty centimetres of the curb, without the car touching any other car or the curb in the process. He or she will complete the task in not more than three manoeuvres, using correct signals and observing all traffic rules. This task will be preformed once each on the left and the right side of the road, and on an uphill and a downhill gradient of between 2 and 10 percent. Front wheels will be turned away from/towards curb on upgrade/downgrade. The driver will meet all the above requirements on at least three of the four attempts and will not touch another car on any attempt. (p. 201)

The point being made here is not that art activities cannot be subjected to such performance criteria, but that the essence of artistic disclosure is rarely captured by positivist models of assessment.

In recent years more attention has been paid to humanistic and naturalistic evaluation models, not only in art education, but within the wider field of educational practice. Evaluators no longer merely inspect schools as disinterested parties, they actively participate in school routines and openly discuss various aspects of professional practice with teachers. Their reports are usually more qualitative than quantitative and focus primarily upon human interactions.

One of the early proponents of humanistic evaluation was Robert Stake (1975), who coined the term *responsive evaluation.* Stake's model was primarily concerned with the assessment of curriculum or programme activities at the school or board level.

The following ten-step model of responsive evaluation is an implementation sequence developed by Ornstein & Hunkins (1993),[150] however, this recent model is a modified version of Robert Stake's original plan. Although described in terms of assessment at the school level, it may also be applied to the evaluation of individual classroom teachers or curricula:

- Negotiate a framework for evaluation with the sponsors.
- Elicit topics, issues, and/or questions of concern from the sponsors.
- Formulate questions for guiding the evaluation.
- Identify the scope and activities of the curriculum; identify the needs of clients and personnel.
- Observe, interview, prepare logs and case studies, and so on.
- Pare down the information; identify the major issues or questions.
- Present initial findings in a tentative report.
- Analyze reactions and investigate predominant concerns more fully.
- Look for conflicting evidence that would invalidate findings, as well as collaborative evidence that would support findings.
- Report the results.

A more recent example of humanistic evaluation is Elliot Eisner's model of *educational connoisseurship*: "the art of appreciating the educationally significant".[151]   Such appreciation is conducted through description, interpretation, and assessment, a process similar to Laura Chapman's model of art criticism presented in *Section 4.2: Planning for Art*:

Eisner's case for educational criticism and connoisseurship draws heavily from the arts. If an individual is to be an illuminating critic of painting, opera, theatre, film, or even wine, he or she must first be a connoisseur - that is, he or she must possess knowledge about and experience with the type of phenomenon he or she is to criticize. A good critic has an awareness and appreciation of the subtle qualities of the situation; he or she can detect and write about the nuances of the situation in ways that help others to become more aware of the phenomenon under consideration. (Ornstein & Hunkins, 1993. p. 339)

Thus, Eisner's concept of educational connoisseurship merges the objective elements of *pedagogic content knowledge* (Shulman, 1987) with the subjective aspects of *pedagogic tact* (Van Manen, 1990, 1991).

Moving to the context of the art studio, **one of the most commonly employed humanistic assessment strategies in art education is the** *nondirective interview* which is designed to help students "strengthen their self-perceptions and evaluate their own progress and development".[152] The nondirective interview typically follows a five stage sequence (Joyce, Weil & Showers, 1992):

Phase One   **Defining the Helping Situation**
The teacher encourages free expression of feelings.

Phase Two   **Exploring the Problem**
The student is encouraged to define the problem. The teacher accepts and clarifies feelings.

Phase Three   **Developing Insight**
The student discusses the problem. The teacher supports the student.

Phase Four   **Planning and Decision Making**
The student plans the initial decision making. The teacher clarifies possible decision.

Phase Five   **Integration**
The student gains further insight and develops more positive actions. The teacher is supportive.

Ronald MacGregor (1990a, 1991, 1992) has suggested the use of *external moderators*, to balance the innately subjective nature of humanistic evaluation:

> Where system-wide criteria are used for assessment, there
> may be instances where individual teachers award marks or
> grades that are too high or too low, relative to those of
> students in other schools within the system. A moderator
> is a person whose role is to adjust marks to ensure an
> equitable distribution among all participating schools.
> (MacGregor, 1992, p. 36)

Moderators are currentlyused for the assessment of student art progress in
the United Kingdom, the Netherlands, Australia, and New Zealand.[153] It
is worth noting that all but one of these countries share a common
educational heritage as members of the former British empire.   The
employment of external moderators for systemic evaluation can be
considered a legacy from the South Kensington school of art education,
exported throughout the empire in the last century.[154]   Canada has not
instituted a similar assessment structure, a fact that probably reflects the
influence American child-centred art theories have had in this country. In
the case of the Netherlands, Dutch art education has long relied on
prescriptive courses of study that ask students to complete studio exercises
within a book-portfolio. These book-portfolios,which allow for more student
creativity than the "copy books" used in Canada before World War I,[155]
subsequently provide the basis for individual art assessment.

Reporting student achievement in art

Once assessment processes have been concluded, teachers need to
report summative evaluations to students, administrators, and parents. This
reporting sequence traditionally begins with the students, who should know
their assessment results almost as soon as their teachers. It usually concludes
with the parents, who are informed of poor student progress so belatedly that
they find it difficult to work effectively as partners with the teachers to
produce positive changes in student performance. This unhelpful sequence
can be altered by reducing the importance of summative evaluations and
increasing the profile of formative assessments.   Formative assessments
facilitate parental involvement in student activities at an early stage and allow
parents to work alongside teachers in addressing student problems long
before they become resistant to remedial action.

As with assessment criteria, **reporting processes should be explicitly
explained to students before activities are begun.**   It is important that
students understand their responsibilities for documenting aspects of work-in-
progress, group contributions,and other formative activities. Students should
be involved in the reporting process wherever appropriate and whenever
possible. This might require the students to maintain studio information
files, personal journals, or daily logs for formative assessment; alternatively,

it might require the students to prepare anecdotal reports or individual evaluation schemes for summative purposes.

Reporting student achievement in art is often inadequately conveyed by quantitative, norm-referenced scales, such as percentages, numerical scores, or alphabetic grades. **Artistic activities are more usefully reported through qualitative, self-referenced measures**, such as anecdotal reports, oral interviews, or checklists that address both the process- and product-based elements of artistic disclosure. Unfortunately, however, such qualitative reports are often belittled by administrators and parents, who favour quantitative formats. Despite the rich mine of information typically offered by qualitative reports, parents and principals seem strangely satisfied with solitary letters of the alphabet or two-digit numbers.

Whatever report formats they select, **teachers should avoid assigning student assessments that they cannot adequately defend**. Students should be given specific attributes that norm-referenced scales would represent. For example, teachers need to be able to describe, in some detail, at least three or four qualities that would distinguish performances warranting a grade of *8 out of 10* from those receiving *6 out of 10*. Similarly, several specific attributes should be outlined that would qualify a painting for an *A* rather than a *B*. If teachers are unable to describe some characteristics that distinguish one discrete grade from another, it would seem prudent to rely upon some other assessment vehicle.

Teachers also need to apply common sense to norm-referenced evaluation schemes, such as percentages. While it is easy to devise marking schemes that add up to *100%*, defending a mark of *72%* over *73%* is simply inappropriate for most art activities. The level of summative precision that percentages imply can rarely be defended in the context of art education. Numerical intervals that offer less precise distinctions, such as percentage intervals (...*70%, 75%, 80%, 85%, ...*) or the numbers *1 through 10* allow for more defensible numerical reporting. Obviously, assessment attributes can never be exhaustively listed, nor can all disclosure-based works be fully anticipated in advance by teachers. Students do need, however, some assessment and reporting parameters from teachers prior to the start of studio activities; art education cannot shine in classrooms where the teachers and students are working in the dark.

Reporting procedures that rely on **qualitative instruments are not exempt from the need for teacher explanations prior to the commencement of student activities**. For example, anecdotal reports or assessment checklists that allude to *creativity* should be founded on straightforward understandings of what is meant by the term. To illustrate this point, the concept of creativity as task analysis[156] could be used to generate at least four different categories of student performance, any one of which could substantiate claims of "highly creative work":

Originality	Mary created a really unique sculpture during her study of farm animals.
Fluency	Steve used four different media within his studio unit on urban crime.
Flexibility	Ken identified similarities among exemplars of native art from several countries that we studied this term.
Elaboration	April produced an abstract watercolour based upon "The Last Supper".

Perhaps the best way to demonstrate artistic achievement to students, administrators, and parents is to provide opportunities for displays. One of the innate strengths of art is its ability to provide physical evidence of student growth. When prudently planned, displays facilitate the celebrative aspect of summative assessment, a quality which is so frequently absent from academic evaluative instruments. Displays also allow students to reveal what they can do both individually and collectively.

There are, however, some aspects of displaying student art work that need to be considered by teachers in advance. First, is there enough space for all student works to be included? In most classroom settings display space is very limited, so the answer to this initial question is probably, no. **If including every child's work is a key objective, the problem can be solved by considering display venues outside of the classroom proper.** There are many auxiliary places within schools that can be used, such as corridors, lunchrooms, lobbies, gyms, staffrooms, and offices. Placing art in these areas encourages students to take pride in their school and fosters a sense of civility in parts of the school that are difficult for teachers to directly supervise. Even if student displays can be accommodated within the school building teachers should consider external venues, such as local hospitals, nursing homes, civic centres, and shopping malls. Such settings provide excellent opportunities to raise levels of public support for art, especially among taxpayers who do not have children in school.

Displaying every piece of student work is not always the best course of action for teachers to take. Teachers need to be aware of the sense of personal ownership that art students feel toward works that they produce; if students ask that their art not be displayed, their wishes should be respected. There are many valid reasons why some student art should not be displayed. For example, students can be subjected to ridicule by classmates if their art is placed alongside more proficient work. Student work can exhibit errors that, if displayed, could be mistakenly repeated by other students. As well, student work may contain deeply personal or offensive subject matter; in such situations, teachers need to consult the student(s) involved before deciding whether or not to display the work.

If not every work is going to be displayed, teachers should explain the selection process to their students at the outset. **Selection processes based upon student competition or teacher partiality should be scrupulously avoided.** Some appropriate selection strategies include:

- asking students to display their own work on a voluntary basis;
- displaying works from preselected students (the first ten students on the class register, students from the two rows of desks closest to the window, et cetera); and,
- displaying works that have most clearly achieved the aims and objectives outlined in the introductory lesson.

When using such approaches, **teachers need to ensure that all students enjoy roughly equal display opportunities**. Equity will be more easily achieved if the art curriculum involves a wide range of studio media and group activities; under such conditions every student will likely produce quality work suitable for display.

One final suggestion regarding art displays: **let students volunteer to put up and take down the displays.** If teachers do all of the work themselves, displays have a tendency to outlive their value. Faded art work speaks volumes.

Displays are not the raisons d'être for art education, but they are the natural expressions of student achievement in art. Professionally handled, they provide a celebratory conclusion to one learning activity and a motivating introduction to the next.

▪ Notes

1. May, 1975, p. 89.
2. See Blackwell, 1989; Chalmers, 1993; Clark, 1991a, 1992b, 1993b; Gidney & Millar, 1990; Marotta, 1993; and Martin, 1991a, 1991b, 1993.
3. See Rogers, 1990.
4. See Pearse, 1992b; and Soucy, 1989.
5. See Chalmers, 1984, 1990; and Soucy & Stankiewicz, 1990.
6. Common schools of the 19th century evolved into contemporary elementary schools.
7. See Blackwell, 1989; Bolin, 1990; and Soucy & Stankiewicz, 1990.
8. Gidney & Millar, 1990, p. 14.
9. See Bolin, 1990; and Stankiewicz, 1992.
10. See Chalmers, 1984, 1990, 1993.
11. See Martin, 1993; and Ontario Ministry of Education, 1986.
12. The history of Beal Secondary School is traced in Goodson & Anstead, 1993. See also Chalmers, 1993.
13. See Marotta, 1993.
14. Gidney & Millar, 1990, p. 246.
15. *Ibid.*, p. 249.
16. *Ibid.*, p. 291.
17. Rogers, 1990, p. 153.
18. Martin, 1993, p. 53.
19. Rogers, 1990, p. 155.
20. *Ibid.*, p. 155.
21. See Gidney & Millar, 1990; Goodson, 1987, 1988; Goodson & Anstead, 1993; Longstreet & Shane, 1993; Marotta, 1993; and Pratt, 1980.
22. Pratt, 1980, p. 26.
23. Efland, 1990b, p. 119.
24. *Ibid.*, p. 118.
25. See Stankiewicz, 1984.
26. See Black, 1986; and Martin, 1990, 1991a.
27. See Bruner, 1960; and Phenix, 1960, 1962.
28. See Ornstein & Hunkins, 1993.
29. Ornstein & Hunkins, 1993, p. 196. Reconceptualists are also discussed at the start of *Chapter 2: Art as a Pedagogic Subculture.*
30. See Kasson, 1981; and Van Manen 1990, 1991.
31. See Lanier 1982, 1990.
32. Bailin, 1993, p. 96.

33. Confluent education is discussed in Efland, 1990a, and Ornstein & Hunkins, 1993.
34. Efland, 1990a, p. 262.
35. Templeton, 1990, p. 31.
36. See Gaitskell, Hurwitz & Day, 1982; Kellogg, 1969; and Lansing, 1969.
37. Lowenfeld & Brittain, 1987, p. 179.
38. See *Section 1.1: Divergent Roots of Art Education* for more information on the use of copy books in early drawing curricula.
39. "Copying and tracing deny the child the opportunity to think, to solve problems, and to develop individual abilities. Also, they do not provide the creative work necessary for the development of the imagination." (CSEA, 1993, p. 22)
40. The importance of antecedent traditions is discussed in Bailin, 1988; and Smith, 1992a, 1992b, 1993.
41. CSEA, 1993, p. 22.
42. See Clark, 1992c.
43. See Bracey, 1990.
44. See Soucy, 1989.
45. See Gidney & Millar, 1990.
46. Existential models of curriculum are discussed within Clark, 1992a, 1992d; Courtney, 1980, 1988, 1989; Goodson, 1987, 1988, 1992, 1993; Longstreet & Shane, 1993; Ornstein & Hunkins, 1993; and Van Manen, 1990, 1991.
47. Efland, 1990b, p. 131.
48. Artistic disclosure is discussed in *Section 3.4: Artistic Disclosure.*
49. The concept of a curricular moment is explained in Courtney, 1980; and Van Manen, 1990, 1991.
50. The notion of teacher's voice is discussed in Butt, Raymond, McCue & Yamagashi, 1992; Goodson & Anstead, 1993; and Snider, 1989.
51. See Pinar, 1988.
52. Huling-Austin & Houston, 1993, p. 93.
53. *Ibid.*, p. 94.
54. See Clark, 1992d.
55. See Ontario Department of Education, 1968.
56. See Ontario Ministry of Education, 1986.
57. See Clark, 1991a, 1992d.
58. See Ontario Ministry of Education, 1990.
59. See Layton, 1972.
60. See Shulman, 1987.
61. See Blomeyer, 1991; Goodson, Mangan & Rhea, 1991; and Gray & MacGregor, 1991.
62. See Clark, 1992d.
63. See Clark, 1993b; and Gidney & Millar, 1990.

64. See Clark, 1991a; Efland, 1990a, 1990b; Irwin, 1991b; and Pratt, 1980.
65. See Courtney, 1980, 1982.
66. Brewer, 1992, p. 3.
67. Martin, 1990, p. 24.
68. See Schwab, 1970.
69. Efland, 1990b, p. 127.
70. Hirst, 1974, p. 133.
71. Philip Phenix's arguments in favour of subject specialists can be found in Ornstein & Hunkins, 1993, p. 159.
72. *Ibid.*
73. Gardner's theory of multiple intelligences is discussed with *Section 3.1: Creativity.*
74. See Efland, 1990b.
75. See Courtney, 1980, 1982, 1989.
76. Courtney, 1988, p.2.
77. See Goodson, Mangan & Rhea, 1991; and Gray, 1981, 1992.
78. For more information about nondirective teaching, see *Section 4.2: Planning for Art.*
79. Bell, 1985, p.9.
80. Case, 1992, p. 33.
81. See Clark, 1990; Elam, 1990; and Pearse, 1992b.
82. See Clark, 1991a; Efland, 1990a; Irwin, 1991b; and Pratt, 1980.
83. Ornstein & Hunkins, 1993, p. 340.
84. Courtney, 1982, p. 155.
85. See Emerson, 1993.
86. Artistic genius is discussed at length in Abra, 1988.
87. See Skinner, 1968, 1974, 1976.
88. Bailin, 1988, p. 129.
89. *Ibid.*, p. 109.
90. For more information about multiple intelligences, see Brandt, 1988; and Gardner, 1983, 1989.
91. For more information about brain hemisphericity, see Edwards, 1979, 1986; Kolb, 1976; and McCarthy, 1980.
92. See Hunt, 1961.
93. See Hodgkinson, 1991.
94. Project Zero is discussed within Brandt, 1988; and Gardner, 1983, 1989.
95. See Abra, 1988.
96. For more information about medical studies conducted on split-brain patients, see Levy, 1968, 1974; and Sperry, 1968, 1973.
97. See Edwards, 1979.
98. Ways of knowing are discussed within Courtney, 1988, 1989; Kolb, 1976; and McCarthy, 1980.

99. Further information regarding learning styles can be found within *Section 4.3: Monitoring Art.*
100. McCarthy's *4MAT* model of curriculum is explained within *Section 4.3: Monitoring Art.*
101. Dreyfus & Dreyfus, 1984, p. 582.
102. See Papert, 1980.
103. The implications for teacher preparation posed by the Dreyfus & Dreyfus model of skill acquisition are discussed in Clark, 1991e.
104. Dreyfus & Dreyfus, 1984, p. 590.
105. The generic skills movement is critiqued in McPeck, 1981; McPeck, Martin, Sanders & Slemon, 1989; and Winne, 1989.
106. Courtney, 1982, p. 72.
107. See Ellis, 1965, 1972.
108. Courtney, 1982, pp. 81-84.
109. See Getty, 1985, 1989.
110. Van Manen, 1990, p. 185.
111. *Ibid.*, 1990, p. 35.
112. See Irwin, 1992a; and MacGregor, 1988.
113. See Courtney, 1980, 1982, 1988, 1989.
114. See Blackwell, 1989; Clark, 1993b; Gidney & Millar, 1990; and Martin, 1993.
115. The emergence of art as a school subject is outlined in *Section 1.1: Divergent Roots of Art Education.*
116. See Clark, 1987, 1990, 1991a, 1992a.
117. See Dudek, 1974; and Kellogg, 1969.
118. The contributions to art education made by Frank Cizek are discussed within Efland, 1990a; and Gaitskell, Hurwitz & Day, 1982.
119. The concept of confluent education is presented in Efland, 1990a; and Ornstein & Hunkins, 1993.
120. See Gaitskell, Hurwitz & Day, 1982; and Lowenfeld & Brittain, 1987.
121. Case, 1992, p. 33.
122. For a deeper understanding of what disclosure implies, see *Section 3.4: Artistic Disclosure.*
123. The notion of teachers as parents is discussed more fully in *Section 3.4: Monitoring Art.*
124. Courtney, 1980, pp. 77-78.
125. See Courtney, 1980; Grambs & Carr, 1991; Huling-Austin & Houston, 1993; Pasch, Sparks-Langer, Gardner, Starko & Moody, 1991; and Pratt, 1980.
126. Ontario Ministry of Education, 1989, pp. 3-4.
127. Pasch, Sparks-Langer, Gardner, Starko & Moody, 1991, p. 4.
128. See Schwab, 1970.
129. Huling-Austin & Houston, 1993, p. 93.

130. See *Chapter 1: Art as an Emergent School Subject.*
131. Issues related to computer-based activities in art education are detailed in Clark, 1991b.
132. See Fast, 1988a, 1988b, 1990.
133. See Bailin, 1988. Bailin's contention that artistic performance operates primarily through logical cognition is discussed more fully within *Section 3.1: Creativity.*
134. See Irwin, 1991a.
135. Bailin, 1988, p. 18.
136. See Irwin, 1992a; and MacGregor, 1988.
137. For specific examples of experiential approaches to art history see Smith, 1993.
138. See Chalmers, 1992; Hamblen, 1986; Mansell, 1991; and MacGregor, 1990b.
139. See Kellogg, 1969; Lansing, 1969; and Lowenfeld & Brittain, 1987).
140. Joyce, Weil & Showers, 1992, pp. 264-265.
141. Van Manen, 1991, p. 18.
142. The theme of pedagogic thoughtfulness is explored in Pearse, 1992a; and Van Manen, 1990, 1991.
143. Pedagogic moments are discussed in Courtney, 1980; and Van Manen, 1991.
144. Joyce, Weil & Showers, 1992, p. 265.
145. For more information about programming for the gifted in art, see Hurwitz, 1983.
146. The principles of developmentalism are discussed within *Section 1.3: Developing Trends in Art Education.*
147. See Rogers, 1961.
148. For more information about studio information files, see Hurwitz, 1983; and Ontario Ministry of Education, 1986.
149. Ornstein & Hunkins, 1993, p. 338.
150. Ornstein & Hunkins, 1993, p. 340. This ten-step model of responsive evaluation is a modified version of Stake's original plan.
151. Eisner, 1993, p. 226.
152. Joyce, Weil & Showers, 1992, p. 264.
153. See MacGregor 1990a, 1991.
154. The South Kensington model is discussed within *Section 1.1: Divergent Roots of Art Education.*
155. See Chalmers, 1990; Rogers, 1990; and Soucy, 1989.
156. See Torrance, 1962.

■ Supplementary Readings

Art Education: *History of,*

Efland, A. (1990). *A history of art education: Intellectual and social currents in teaching the visual arts.* New York, NY: Teachers College Press.
MacGregor, R. (Ed.). (1984). *Readings in Canadian art education.* Vancouver, B.C.: Pacific Educational Press.
Soucy, D. & Stankiewicz, M. (Eds.). (1990). *Framing the past: Essays on art education.* Reston, VA: National Art Education Association.

Art Education: *Methods of,*

Gaitskell, C.D., Hurwitz, A. & Day, M. (1982). *Children and their art: Methods for the elementary school* (4th ed.). Toronto, Ont.: Harcourt Brace Jovanovich, Inc.
Herberholz, B. & Hanson, L. (1990). *Early childhood art* (4th ed.). Dubuque, IA: Wm. C. Brown.
Herberholz, D. & Herberholz, B. (1990). *Artworks for elementary teachers: Developing artistic and perceptual awareness* (6th ed.). Dubuque, IA: Wm. C. Brown.
Hurwitz, A. (1983). *The gifted and talented in art: A guide to program planning.* Worcester, MA: Davis.
Linderman, M. (1984). *Art in the elementary school* (3rd ed.). Dubuque, IA: Wm. C. Brown.
Lowenfeld, V. & Brittain, W. (1987). *Creative and mental growth* (8th ed.). London, UK: Macmillan.
MacGregor, R. (1977). *Art plus.* Toronto, Ont.: McGraw-Hill.
Schirrmacher, R. (1993). *Art and creative development for young children* (2nd ed.). Albany, NY: Delmar.

Art Education: *Theories of,*

Eisner, E. (1972). *Educating artistic vision.* New York, NY: Macmillan.
_____. (1993). *Educational imagination: On the design and evaluation of school programs* (3rd ed.). New York, NY: Macmillan.
Feldman, E. (1987). *Varieties of visual experience* (3rd ed.). Englewood Cliffs, NJ: Prentice-Hall.
Getty Center for Education in the Arts. (1989). *Inheriting the theory: New voices and multiple perspectives on DBAE.* Los Angeles, CA: Author.

Kellogg, R. (1969). *Analyzing children's art.* Palo Alto, CA: National Press Books.

Lanier, V. (1982). *The arts we see.* New York, NY: Teachers College Press.

Read, H. (1943). *Education through art.* London, UK: Faber and Faber.

Art Education: *Textbooks/Kits*

Chapman, L. (1987). *Discover art* (rev. ed.). Worcester, MA: Davis.

_____. (1989). *Teaching art: Grades 1-3.* Worcester, MA: Davis.

_____. (1989). *Teaching art: Grades 4-6.* Worcester, MA: Davis.

_____. (1992). *A world of images.* Worcester, MA: Davis.

Deans, D. (1992). *In the mind's eye.* Mississauga, Ont.: Copp Clark Pitman, Ltd.

Hubbard, G. (1987). *Art in action.* San Diego, CA: Coronado.

Hubel, V. & Lussow, D. (1984). *Focus on designing.* Toronto, Ont.: McGraw-Hill Ryerson Ltd.

Mittler, G. (1986). *Art in focus.* Peoria, Ill: Bennett & McKnight Publishing Company.

Mittler, G. & Ragans, R. (1992). *Exploring art.* Columbus, OH: Glencoe.

_____. (1992). *Understanding art.* Columbus, OH: Glencoe.

Rissover, F. & Birch, D. (1983). *Mass media and the popular press* (3rd ed.). Toronto, Ont.: McGraw-Hill.

Art History

Bennett, B. & Hall, C. (1984). *Discovering Canadian art: Learning the language.* Scarborough, Ont.: Prentice-Hall.

Brommer, G. (1988). *Discovering art history* (2nd ed.). Worcester, MA: Davis.

Cornell, S. (1983). *Art: A history of changing style.* Englewood Cliffs, NJ: Prentice-Hall.

Feldman, E. (1982). *The artist.* Englewood Cliffs, NJ: Prentice-Hall.

Fleming, W. (1991). *Arts and ideas* (8th ed.). Toronto, Ont.: Holt, Rinehart and Winston, Inc.

Gombrich, E. (1982). *The story of art* (13th ed.). Englewood Cliffs, NJ: Prentice-Hall.

Janson, H.W. (1986). *A basic history of art* (2nd ed.). New York, NY: Harry N. Abrams, Inc.

MacGregor, R., Hall, C., Bennett, B. & Calvert, A. (1987). *Canadian art: Building a heritage.* Scarborough, Ont.: Prentice-Hall.

Curriculum Theory

Courtney, R. (1982). *The dramatic curriculum*. Vancouver, B.C.: Pacific Educational Press.

_____. (1982). *Re-play: Studies of human drama in education*. Toronto, Ont.: OISE Press.

_____. (1989). *Play, drama & thought: The intellectual background to dramatic education* (4th ed.). Toronto, Ont.: Simon & Pierre.

Fogarty, R. (1991). *How to integrate the curricula: The mindful school* (Series). Palatine, ILL: Skylight.

Gardner, H. (1983). *Frames of mind: The theory of multiple intelligences*. New York, NY: Basic Books.

Gidney, R. & Millar, W. (1990). *Inventing secondary education: The rise of the high school in nineteenth-century Ontario*. Montreal, Que.: McGill-Queen's University Press.

Goodson, I. (1987). *School subjects and curriculum change: Studies in curriculum history* (rev. ed.). London, UK: Falmer Press.

_____. (Ed.). (1988). *The making of curriculum: Collected essays*. Philadelphia, PA: Falmer Press.

_____. (Ed.). (1992). *Studying teachers' lives*. New York, NY: Teachers College Press.

Joyce, B., Weil, M. & Showers, B. (1992). *Models of teaching* (4th ed.). Boston, MA: Allyn & Bacon.

Longstreet, W. & Shane, H. (1993). *Curriculum for a new millenium*. Toronto, Ont.: Allyn and Bacon.

McCarthy, B. (1981). *The 4MAT system: Teaching to learning styles with right/left mode techniques* (2nd ed.). Barrington, ILL: Excel, Inc.

Ornstein, A. & Hunkins, F. (1993). *Curriculum: Foundations, principles, and theory* (2nd ed.). Toronto, Ont.: Allyn and Bacon.

Van Manen, M. (1991). *The tact of teaching: The meaning of pedagogical thoughtfulness*. London, Ont.: Althouse Press.

Other Books of Interest to Art Teachers

Bailin, S. (1988). *Achieving extraordinary ends: An essay on creativity*. Norwell, MA: Kluwer Academic Publishers.

Brewer, J. (1992). *Introduction to early childhood education: Preschool through primary grades*. Toronto, Ont.: Allyn and Bacon.

Collins, G. & Sandell, R. (1984). *Women, art and education*. Reston, VA: National Art Education Association.

Courtney, R. (1987). *The quest: Research & inquiry in arts education*. Lanham, MD: University Press of America.

Edwards, B. (1979). *Drawing on the right side of the brain.* Los Angeles, CA: J.P. Tarcher.

_____. (1986). *Drawing on the artist within: A guide to innovation, invention, imagination and creativity.* New York, NY: Simon & Schuster.

May, R. (1975). *The courage to create.* New York, NY: W.W. Norton.

Qualley, C. (1986). *Safety in the artroom.* Worcester, MA: Davis.

■ References

Abra, J. (1988). Is creative ability widespread? *Canadian Review of Art Education, 15*(2), 69-89.

Abrahams, C. (1986). The fine art subculture in higher education as cultural patriarch to art knowledge in schools. *Journal of Multi-cultural and Cross-cultural Research in Art Education, 4*(1), 64-68.

American Alliance for Theatre and Education, Music Educators National Conference & National Art Education Association. (1991). *National arts education accord: A statement on arts education to governors and state legislators.* Reston, VA: Authors.

Anderson, H. (1965). On the meaning of creativity. In H. Anderson (Ed.), *Creativity in childhood and adolescence* (pp. 46-61). Palo Alto, CA: Science and Behaviour Books.

Arts, Education and Americans Panel. (1977). *Coming to our senses: The significance of the arts for American education.* New York, NY: McGraw-Hill.

Bailey, L. (1920). *The nature study idea.* New York: Macmillan. (Original work published 1903).

Bailin, S. (1988). *Achieving extraordinary ends: An essay on creativity.* Norwell, MA: Kluwer Academic Publishers.

_____. (1993). Drama as experience: A critical view. *Canadian Journal of Education, 18*(2), 95-105.

Barrow, R. (1984). *Giving teaching back to teachers: A critical introduction to curriculum theory.* London, Ont.: Althouse Press.

Baxter, L. (1987). A national art education policy for Canada. *Canadian Review of Art Education, 14*, 35-48.

Bell, R. (1985). The educational arts: The relationship of arts exposure to instructional programs. *Design for Arts in Education*, May/June, p. 10-12.

Bell, C. (1958). *Art.* New York, NY: Capricorn Books.

Bergson, H. (1911). *Laughter* (C. Brereton & F. Rothwell, Trans.). New York, NY: Macmillan.

Black, S. (1986). Herbert Read: His contribution to art education and to education through art. *Journal of the Canadian Society for Education through Art, 17*, 31-34.

Blackwell, R. (1989). The visual arts in general education in Ontario: Whither and especially whence. *Journal of the Ontario Society for Education through Art, 18*, 17-30.

Blomeyer, R. (1991). A case study of microcomputers in art education. In I.F. Goodson & J.M. Mangan (Eds.), *Computers, classrooms, and culture: Studies in the use of computers for classroom learning* (pp.

191-238). London, Ont.: RUCCUS, Faculty of Education, The University of Western Ontario.

Bolin, P. (1990). The Massachusetts drawing act of 1870: Industrial mandate or democratic manoeuvre? In D. Soucy & M. Stankiewicz (Eds.), *Framing the past: Essays on art education* (pp. 59-70). Reston, VA: National Art Education Association.

Board of Education for the City of Etobicoke (Ontario). (1987). *Making the grade: Evaluating student progress.* Scarborough, Ont.: Prentice-Hall.

Bracey, E. (1990). Art education for the 2020s: One that is truly moral. *Canadian Review of Art Education, 17*(1), 37-49.

Brameld, T. (1950). *Patterns of educational philosophy.* Yonkers, NY: World Book.

Brandt, R. (1988). On assessment in the arts: A conversation with Howard Gardner. *Educational Leadership, 45*(4), 30-34.

Brewer, J. (1992). *Introduction to early childhood education: Preschool through primary grades.* Toronto, Ont.: Allyn and Bacon.

Broudy, H. (1976). Impression and expression in artistic development. In E. Eisner (Ed.), *The arts, human development and education* (pp. 87-97). Berkeley, CA: McCutchan.

Bruner, J. (1960). *The process of education.* Cambridge, MA: Harvard University Press.

Bullock, A. & Galbraith, L. (1992). Images of art teaching: Comparing the beliefs and practices of two secondary art teachers. *Studies in Art Education, 33*(2), 86-97.

Bullough, E. (1959). Psychical distance as a factor in art and aesthetic principle. In M. Weitz (Ed.), *Problems in aesthetics* (pp. 646-658). New York, NY: Macmillan.

Butt, R., Raymond, D., McCue, G. & Yamagishi, L. (1992). Collaborative autobiography and the teacher's voice. In I. F. Goodson (Ed.), *Studying teachers' lives* (pp. 51-98). New York, NY: Teachers College Press.

Canadian Society for Education through Art. (1993). CSEA policy statement #3: A statement of policy regarding the use of non-creative commercially-prepared devices. *CSEA Newsletter, 36*(3), 22.

Case, R. (1992). The anatomy of curricular integration. *The Recorder, 35*(1), 30-36.

Chalmers, F.G. (1978). Teaching and studying art history: Some anthropological and sociological considerations. *Studies in Art Education, 20*(1), 18-25.

_____. (1984). South Kensington and the colonies: David Blair of New Zealand and Canada. *Studies in Art Education, 26*(2), 69-74.

_____. (1990). South Kensington in the farthest colony. In D. Soucy & M. Stankiewicz (Eds.), *Framing the past: Essays on art education* (pp. 71-86). Reston, VA: National Art Education Association.

_____. (1992). The origins of racism in the public school art curriculum. *Studies in Art Education, 33*(3), 134-143.

_____. (1993). Who is to do this great work for Canada? South Kensington in Ontario. *Journal of Art & Design Education, 12*(2), 161-178.

Chandler, A. (1966). Types of listeners. In E. Vivas & M. Kriegar (Eds.), *The problems of aesthetics* (pp. 290-296).

Chapman, L. (1992). *A world of images.* Worcester, MA: Davis.

Clark, R. (1987). *Aesthetic self-disclosure in visual arts.* Unpublished doctoral dissertation. University of Toronto.

_____. (1990). Student disclosure: A new conceptual framework for art curricula. *Journal of the Ontario Society for Education through Art, 19*, 35-43.

_____. (1991a). Art as an emergent school subject: Perspectives and a proposal from Ontario. *Studies in Art Education, 32*(4), 220-229.

_____. (1991b). Computer-based activities in art education: Impetus and impediments. In I.F. Goodson & J.M. Mangan (Eds.), *RUCCUS occasional papers, Vol. 2* (pp. 145-190). London, Ont.: Research Unit on Classroom Learning and Computer Use in Schools, Faculty of Education, University of Western Ontario.

_____. (1991c). Enduring constants and emerging conflicts: Art education in Ontario, 1980-1990. *Journal of the Ontario Society for Education through Art, 20*, 31-38.

_____. (1991d). Principal investigator's report: Art. In I. Goodson, M. Mangan, & V. Rhea (Eds.), *Curriculum and context in the use of computers for classroom learning: Summative report, Volume 2* (pp. 14-82). London, Ont.: Faculty of Education, University of Western Ontario.

_____. (1991e). Student teachers and educational theory: Say goodbye...for now. *Journal of the Canadian Society for Education through Art, 22*(1), 19-22.

_____. (1992a). Aesthetic self-disclosure in art. *Canadian Review of Art Education, 19*(1), 48-59.

_____. (1992b). Enduring constants and emerging conflicts: Art education in Ontario, 1980-1990. *Journal of the Canadian Society for Education through Art, 23*(1), 23-27.

_____. (1992c). Fundamentalists in the classroom: The special needs of the well-behaved child. *Journal of the Ontario Society for Education through Art, 21*, 35-48.

_____. (1992d). Art as a pedagogic subculture: Fixing the leaky roof of educational reform. *Canadian Review of Art Education, 19*(2), 102-113.

_____. (1993a). Beyond visual arts: The importance of nomenclature. *Journal of the Canadian Society for Education through Art, 24*(1). 12-16.

_____. (1993b). Common, superior, and accomplishments: The roots of art education in Ontario curricula. *Journal of the Ontario Society for Education through Art, 22*, 35-45.

Cole, A. (1991). Interviewing for life history: A process of ongoing negotiation. In I.F. Goodson, J.M. Mangan (Eds.), *Qualitative educational research studies: Methodologies in transition* (pp. 185-208). London, Ont.: RUCCUS, Faculty of Education, The University of Western Ontario.

Collins, G. & Sandell, R. (1984). *Women, art and education.* Reston, VA: National Art Education Association.

_____. (1987). Women's achievements in art: An issues approach for the classroom. *Art Education, 40*(3), 12-21.

Cormack, W. (1991). On the struggle for school-based arts. *Design for Arts in Education, 92*(3), 40-45.

Courtney, R. (1980). *The dramatic curriculum.* Vancouver, B.C.: Pacific Educational Press.

_____. (1982). *Re-play: Studies of human drama in education.* Toronto, Ont.: OISE Press.

_____. (1988). *No one way of being: A study of the practical knowledge of elementary arts teachers* (Contract 0634 ON03699). Toronto, Ont.: Ontario Ministry of Government Services (MGS) Publications Services.

_____. (1989). *Play, drama & thought: The intellectual background to dramatic education* (4th ed., rev.). Toronto, Ont.: Simon & Pierre.

Denton, D. (1979). *Concepts and strategies of phenomenological research.* Paper presented to the American Educational Research Association, San Francisco, California.

Dewey, J. (1916). *Democracy and education.* New York, NY: Macmillan.

Dollard, J. & Miller, N. (1950). *Personality and psychotherapy.* New York, NY: McGraw-Hill.

Dondis, D. (1973). *A primer of visual literacy.* Cambridge, MA: M.I.T. Press.

Doyle, C. (1971, September). *Honesty as a structurally necessary aspect of the creative process.* Paper presented to the American Psychological Association, Washington, D.C. (ERIC Document Reproduction Service No. ED 058 582)

Dreyfus, H. & Dreyfus, S. (1984). Putting computers in their proper place: Analysis versus intuition in the classroom. *Teachers College Record, 85*(4), 578-601.

Dudek, S. (1974). Creativity in young children - attitude or ability? *Journal of Creative Behaviour, 4,* 282-292.

Duncum, P. (1990). Clearing the decks for dominant culture: Some first principles for a contemporary art education. *Studies in Art Education, 31*(4), 207-215.

Ecker, D. (1963). The artistic process as qualitative problem solving. *Journal of Aesthetics and Art Criticism, 21*(3), 283-290.

Edwards, B. (1979). *Drawing on the right side of the brain.* Los Angeles, CA: J.P. Tarcher.

_____. (1986). *Drawing on the artist within: A guide to innovation, invention, imagination and creativity.* New York, NY: Simon & Schuster.

Efland, A. (1990a). *A history of art education: Intellectual and social currents in teaching the visual arts.* New York, NY: Teachers College Press.

_____. (1990b). Art education in the twentieth century: A history of ideas. In D. Soucy & M. Stankiewicz (Eds.), *Framing the past: Essays on art education* (pp. 117-136). Reston, VA: National Art Education Association.

Eisner, E. (1972). *Educating artistic vision.* New York, NY: Macmillan.

_____. (1985). Why art in education and why art education? In L.L. Duke (Ed.), *Beyond creating: The place for art in America's schools* (pp. 64-69). Los Angeles, CA: Getty Center for Education in the Arts.

_____. (1993). *Educational imagination: On the design and evaluation of school programs* (3rd ed.). New York, NY: Macmillan.

Elam, S. (1990, September). The 22nd annual Gallup Poll of the public's attitudes toward the public schools. *Kappan, 72*(1), pp. 41-55.

Ellis, H. (1965). *Transfer of learning.* New York, NY: Macmillan.

_____. (1972). *Fundamentals of human learning and cognition.* Dubuque, IA: Wm. C. Brown.

Emerson, J. (1993, May). Art education in transition. *CSEA Newsletter, 36*(2), pp. 3-4.

Fast, L. (1988a). Notes to pre-service teachers on preliminary planning for lessons in visual arts. *Journal of the Ontario Society for Education through Art, 17,* 32-35.

_____. (1988b). A rationale and practical applications for illustration of written text in elementary school art programs. *Journal of the Ontario Society for Education through Art, 17,* 36-39.

_____. (1989). In praise of repetition. *Journal of the Ontario Society for Education through Art, 18,* 52-53.

_____. (1990). The hidden messages in using pupil art for classroom decoration. *Journal of the Ontario Society for Education through Art, 19*, 32-34.

Feldman, E. (1982). *The artist.* Englewood Cliffs, NJ.: Prentice-Hall.

_____. (1987). *Varieties of visual experience* (3rd ed.). Englewood Cliffs, NJ: Prentice-Hall.

_____. (1989). The centrality of art criticism. *Journal of the Canadian Society for Education through Art, 20*(1), 9-13.

Flanagan, J. (1963). The definition and measurement of ingenuity. In C. Taylor & F. Barron (Eds.), *Scientific creativity: Its recognition and development* (pp. 89-98). New York, NY: Wiley.

Fogarty, R. (1991a). *How to integrate the curricula: The mindful school* (Series). Palatine, Ill.: Skylight.

_____. (1991b, October). Ten ways to integrate curriculum. *Educational Leadership,* 61-65.

Fry, R. (1956). *Vision and design.* Cleveland, OH: Meridian.

Gaitskell, C.D. (1949). *Arts and crafts in the schools of Ontario.* Ontario Department of Education. Toronto, Ont.: Ryerson.

Gaitskell, C.D., Hurwitz, A. & Day, M. (1982). *Children and their art: Methods for the elementary school* (4th ed.). Toronto, Ont.: Harcourt Brace Jovanovich, Inc.

Garber, E. (1990). Implications of feminist art criticism for art education. *Studies in Art Education, 32*(1), 17-26.

Gardner, H. (1983). *Frames of mind: The theory of multiple intelligences.* New York, NY: Basic Books.

_____. (1989). Zero-based arts education: An introduction to ARTS PROPEL. *Studies in Art Education, 30*(2), 71-83.

Getty Center for Education in the Arts. (1985). *Beyond creating: The place for art in America's schools.* Los Angeles, CA: Author.

_____. (1989). *Inheriting the theory: New voices and multiple perspectives on DBAE.* Los Angeles, CA: Author.

Getzels, J. & Jackson, P. (1962). *Creativity and intelligence.* New York, NY: Wiley.

Gidney, R. & Millar, W. (1990). *Inventing secondary education: The rise of the high school in nineteenth-century Ontario.* Montreal, Que.: McGill-Queen's University Press.

Gilbert, R. (1992). Curriculum integration: Its meaning and its value. *The Recorder, 35*(1), 25-29.

Goodson, I. (1987). *School subjects and curriculum change: Studies in curriculum history* (rev. ed.). London, UK: Falmer Press.

_____. (Ed.). (1988). *The making of curriculum: Collected essays.* Philadelphia, PA: Falmer Press.

_____. (Ed.). (1992). *Studying teachers' lives.* New York, NY: Teachers College Press.

_____. (1993). Status versus significance in school subject knowledge: The Janus face of art education. *Journal of the Ontario Society for Education through Art, 22,* 17-25.

Goodson, I. & Anstead, C. (1993). *Education for efficiency: Representations of the early life of a school.* Toronto, Ont.: Garamond Press.

Goodson, I.F., Mangan, J.M., & Rhea, V. (Eds.). (1991). Closing the circle: Conclusions and recommendations. *Curriculum and context in the use of computers for classroom learning: Summative report, Volume 3.* London, Ont.: RUCCUS, The Faculty of Education, The University of Western Ontario.

Gordon, J. (1961). *Synectics: The development of creative capacity.* New York, NY: Harper & Row.

Grambs, J. & Carr, J. (1991). *Modern methods in secondary education* (5th ed.). Fort Worth, TX: Holt, Rinehart and Winston.

Gray, J. (1981). Which needs changing the most in art education: The preaching or the teaching? *NSCAD Papers in Art Education, 1,* 51-63.

_____. (1992). An art teacher is an art teacher is an art teacher...fortunately! *Art Education, 45*(4), 19-23.

Gray, J. & MacGregor, R. (1990a). PROACTA II: Personally relevant observations about art concepts and teaching activities (Eastern Canada). *Canadian Review of Art Education, 17*(2), 129-135.

_____. (1990b). *A report on the status of art teaching: PROACTA plus.* Unpublished report to the Social Sciences & Humanities Research Council of Canada, December 1990.

_____. (1991). A cross-Canada study of high school art teachers. *Canadian Journal of Education, 16*(1), 47-57.

Gruber, H. (1980). The evolving systems approach to creativity. In S. Modgil & C. Modgil (Eds.), *Toward a theory of psychological development.* Atlantic Highlands, NJ: Humanities Press.

Guilford, J. (1950). Creativity. *American Psychologist, 5,* 444-454.

_____. (1967). *The nature of human intelligence.* New York, NY: McGraw-Hill.

Habermas, J. (1971). *Knowledge and human interests.* Boston, MA: Beacon.

Hamblen, K. (1986). A universal-relative approach to the study of cross-cultural art. *Journal of Multi-cultural and Cross-cultural Research in Art Education, 4*(1), 69-77.

_____. (1988). Approaches to aesthetics in art education: A critical theory perspective. *Studies in Art Education, 29* (2), 81-90.

Hamblen, K. & Galanes, C. (1991). Instructional options for aesthetics: Exploring the possibilities. *Art Education, 44*(6), 12-24.

Harris, W. (1897). Why art and literature ought to be studied in our schools. *Addresses and Proceedings of the NEA,* 261-80.

Herberholz, B. & Hanson, L. (1990). *Early childhood art* (4th ed.). Dubuque, IA: Wm. C. Brown.

Heidegger, M. (1962). *Being and time* (J. Macquarrie & E. Robinson, Trans.). New York, NY: Harper.

Hirst, P. (1974). *Knowledge and the curriculum.* London, UK: Routledge & Kegan Paul.

_____. (1978). *Knowledge and the curriculum: A collection of philosophical papers.* London, UK: Routledge & Kegan Paul.

Hodgkinson, H. (1991). Reform versus reality. *Kappan, 73*(1), 8-16.

Horner, S. (1988). *2b and not 2c: That is not the question.* Unpublished manuscript.

Huling-Austin, L. & Houston, W.R. (1993). Diverse processes in studying teaching: Overview and framework. In M. O'Hair & S. Odell (Eds.), *Diversity and teaching: Teacher education yearbook I* (pp. 91-97). Toronto, Ont.: Harcourt Brace Jovanovich College Publishers.

Hunt, J. (1961). *Intelligence and experience.* New York, NY: Ronald Press.

Hurwitz, A. (1983). *The gifted and talented in art: A guide to program planning.* Worcester, MA: Davis.

Husserl, E. (1913). *Ideas* (W. Boyce Gibson, Trans.). New York, NY: Humanities Press.

Irwin, R. (1991a). Translating the essence of the arts through three curriculum perspectives. *Journal of the Ontario Society for Education through Art, 20,* 50-57.

_____. (1991b). Art education curriculum documents in transition: The shifting currents of change. *Canadian Review of Art Education, 18*(1), 33-44.

_____. (1992a). Weaving the threads of creative expression. *Journal of the Ontario Society for Education through Art, 21,* 24-34.

_____. (1992b). Reflections on the '80s and insight for the '90s: Art education across Canada. *Journal of the Canadian Society for Education through Art, 23*(1), 44-46.

_____. (1992c). A profile of an arts supervisor: A political image. *Studies in Art Education, 33*(2), 110-121.

Jalongo, M. (1990, Summer). The child's right to the expressive arts: Nurturing the imagination as well as the intellect. A position paper of the Association for Childhood Education International. *Childhood Education, 66,* 195-201.

Jourard, S. (1958). Some factors in self-disclosure. *Journal of Abnormal and Social Psychology, 56,* 91-98.

_____. (1971). *Self-disclosure: An experimental analysis of the transparent self.* New York, NY: Wiley-Interscience.

Joyce, B., Weil, M., & Showers, B. (1992). *Models of teaching* (4th ed.). Boston, MA: Allyn & Bacon.

Kakas, K. (1991). Classroom communication during fifth-grade students' drawing lessons: Student-student and student-teacher conversations. *Studies in Art Education, 33*(1), 21-35.

Kampf, L. (1973). Understanding the concrete needs of the historical moment. *Arts in Society, 10,* 63-68.

Kasson, C. (1981, November). *Expression of emotions through art: A phenomenological approach.* Paper presented to the American Educational Studies Association, Boston, Mass. (ERIC Document Reproduction Service No. ED 219 289)

Kellogg, R. (1969). *Analyzing children's art.* Palo Alto, CA: National Press Books.

Kemmis, S., Atkin, R. & Wright, E. (1977). *Working papers on the UNCAL evaluation studies (Occasional Publications No. 5).* Norwich, UK: Centre for Applied Research in Education, University of East Anglia.

Kierkegaard, S. (1959). *A Kierkegaard anthology* (R. Bretall, Ed.). New York, NY: Modern Library.

Kindler, A. (1992). Worship of creativity and artistic development of young children. *Journal of the Canadian Society for Education through Art, 23*(2), 12-16.

King, A. (1981). *Aesthetic response: An overview of selected theories and the postulation of a model.* Unpublished doctoral dissertation. University of California, San Bernadino. (ERIC Document Reproduction Service No. ED 228 567)

King, I. (1991). In search of Lowenfeld's proof that coloring books are harmful to children. *Studies in Art Education, 33*(1), 36-42.

Kolb, D. (1976). *A learning style inventory.* Boston, MA: McBer & Company.

Lanier, V. (1982). *The arts we see.* New York, NY: Teachers College Press, Columbia University.

_____. (1990). The future is behind us. *Canadian Review of Art Education, 17*(1), 51-62.

Lansing, K. (1969). *Art, artists, and art education.* New York, NY: McGraw-Hill.

Layton, D. (1972, January). Science as general education. *Trends in education.*

Levy, J. (1968). Differential perceptual capacities in major and minor hemispheres. *Proceedings of the National Academy of Science, 61,* 1151.

_____. (1974). Psychobiological implications of bilateral asymmetry. In S.J. Diamond & J.G. Beaumont (Eds.), *Hemisphere function in the human brain.* New York, NY: John Wiley and Sons.

Longstreet, W. & Shane, H. (1993). *Curriculum for a new millennium.* Toronto, Ont.: Allyn and Bacon.

Lowenfeld, V. & Brittain, W. (1987). *Creative and mental growth* (8th ed.). London, UK: Macmillan.

MacDonald, B., Atkin, R., Jenkins, D. & Kemmis, S. (1977). *Final report: Understanding computer assisted learning (UNCAL) project*. Norwich, UK: University of East Anglia.

MacGregor, R. (1979). Art education and cultural priorities: The case for feeling special. *Image, 5*, 2-8.

_____. (Ed.). (1984). *Readings in Canadian art education*. Vancouver, B.C.: Pacific Education Press.

_____. (1988). Living traditions: Art history in the school. *Journal of the Ontario Society for Education through Art, 17*, 20-31.

_____. (1990a). *Art assessment in Britain*. Report to the Ministry of Education, British Columbia.

_____. (1990b). Towards 2020: Future directions in art education. *Canadian Review of Art Education, 17*(1), 19-27.

_____. (1991). *Art assessment in South Australia, Victoria and New Zealand*. Report to the Ministry of Education, British Columbia.

_____. (1992). A short guide to alternative assessment practices. *Art Education, 45*(6), 34-38.

MacKinnon, D. (1961). Characteristics of the creative person: Implications for the teaching-learning process. In G. Smith (Ed.), *Current issues in higher education* (pp. 89-92). Washington, DC: Association for Higher Learning.

_____. (1967). The study of creative persons: A method and some results. In J. Kagan (Ed.), *Creativity and learning* (pp. 20-35). Boston, MA.: Houghton Miflin.

Maltzman, I. (1960). On the training of originality. *Psychological Review, 67*, 229-242.

Mansell, A. (1991). Voice of art: Education/image/culture. *Journal of the Ontario Society for Education through Art, 20*, 23-29.

Marotta, M. (1993). *A school for the arts in Ontario: Development and rationales*. Unpublished master's thesis, The University of Western Ontario, London, Ontario.

Martin, J. (1990). Herbert Read: Responses to his conception of an education through art. *Journal of the Ontario Society for Education through Art, 19*, 24-31.

_____. (1991a). Education through art: A method. *Journal of the Ontario Society for Education through Art, 20*, 39-49.

_____. (1991b). Why teach art? Herbert Read's early essays on the revolutionary significance of an education through art. *Canadian Review of Art Education, 18*(2), 136-150.

_____. (1993). Plain, bold and practical: Drawing within a system of public instruction. *Journal of the Ontario Society for Education through Art, 22*, 46-55.

Maslow, A. (1954). *Motivation and personality.* New York, NY: Harper & Brothers.

_____. (1959a). Cognition of being in the peak experiences. *Journal of Genetic Psychology, 94,* 43-66.

_____.(1959b). Creativity in self-actualizing people. In H. Anderson (Ed.), *Creativity and its cultivation* (pp. 83-95). New York, NY: Harper.

Matoba, K. (1985). Little league and child art. *Art Education, 38*(4), 30-31, 46.

Mattil, E. (Ed.). (1966). *A seminar in art education for research and curriculum development.* University Park, PA: Pennsylvania State University.

May, R. (1969). *Love and will.* New York, NY: Dell Publishing Co.

_____. (1975). *The courage to create.* New York, NY: W.W. Norton.

McCarthy, B. (1981). *The 4MAT system: Teaching to learning styles with right/left mode techniques* (2nd ed.). Barrington, Ill: Excel, Inc.

McIntosh, D., Hanley, B., Verriour, P. & Van Gyn, G. (1993). *The state of the art.* Victoria, B.C.: Beach Holme Publisher.

McPeck, J. (1981). *Critical thinking and education.* New York, NY: St. Martin's Press.

McPeck, J., Martin, J., Sanders, J. & Slemon, A. (1989). Aerobics for the mind? *Interchange. 20*(3), 35-38.

McPherson, J. (1963). A proposal for establishing ultimate criteria for measuring creative output. In C. Taylor & F. Barron (Eds.), *Scientific creativity: Its recognition and development* (pp. 24-29). New York, NY: Wiley.

Mednick, S. (1962). The associative basis of the creative process. *Psychological Review, 69,* 220-232.

Miller, J., Cassie, J. & Drake, S. (1990). *Holistic learning: A teacher's guide to integrated studies.* Toronto, Ont.: OISE Press.

Montessori, M. (1964). *The Montessori method.* New York, NY: Schocken Books.

Moody, L. (1992). An analysis of drawing programs for early adolescents. *Studies in Art Education, 34*(1), 39-47.

Mukerjee, R. (1954). *The social function of art.* New York, NY: Philosophical Library.

Mullen, C. & Chalmers, G. (1990). Guest editorial: Culture, society, and art education. *Studies in Art Education, 31*(4), 195-197.

National Education Association. (1894). *Report of the Committee of Ten on Secondary School Studies.* Chicago, Ill: The American Company.

Ontario Department of Education. (1968). *Living and learning: The report of the provincial committee on aims and objectives of education in the schools of Ontario.* Toronto, Ont.: Author.

Ontario Ministry of Education. (1984). *Ontario schools: Intermediate and senior divisions.* Toronto, Ont.: Author.

_____. (1986). *Visual arts: Intermediate and senior divisions.* Toronto, Ont.: Author.

_____. (1989). *Ontario schools: Intermediate and senior divisions* (Rev. ed.). Toronto, Ont.: Author.

_____. (1990). *OAC visual arts examination review.* Toronto, Ont.: Author.

Ontario Ministry of Education and Training. (1993a). *The common curriculum, grades 1-9.* Toronto, Ont.: Author.

_____. (1993b). *Towards an integrated curriculum: A school resource guide.* Toronto, Ont.: Author.

Ontario Music Educators' Association. (1992). Transition years arts models: A rationale. *The Recorder, 35*(1), 23-24.

Ornstein, A. & Hunkins, F. (1993). *Curriculum: Foundations, principles, and theory* (2nd ed.). Toronto, Ont.: Allyn and Bacon.

Osborn, A. (1957). *Applied imagination.* New York, NY: Scribner's.

Papert, S. (1980). *Mindstorms: Children, computers, and powerful ideas.* New York, NY: Harper & Row.

Parsons, M. (1986). The place of a cognitive approach to aesthetic response. *Journal of Aesthetic Education, 20,* 107-111.

Pasch, M., Sparks-Langer, G., Gardner, T., Starko, A. & Moody, C. (1991). *Teaching as decision-making: Instructional practices for the successful teacher.* New York, NY: Longman.

Pearse, H. (1992a). The lost art of pedagogy: An exploration in three parts (Part one: What is pedagogy anyway?). *Canadian Review of Art Education, 16*(1), 60-63.

_____. (1992b). The first to go: Message or myth? *NSCAD Papers in Art Education, 6,* 85-90.

_____. (1992c). Beyond paradigms: Art education theory and practice in a postparadigmatic world. *Studies in Art Education, 33*(4), 244-252.

Phenix, P. (1960). *Realms of meaning.* New York, NY: McGraw-Hill.

_____. (1962). The uses of the disciplines of curriculum content. *Educational Forum, 26*(3), 273-280.

Piaget, J. (1952). *The origins of intelligence in children.* New York, NY: International University Press.

Pinar, W. (1988). Autobiography and the architecture of self. *Journal of Curriculum Theorizing, 8*(1), 7-36.

Pratt, D. (1980). *Curriculum: Design and development.* New York, NY: Harcourt, Brace, Jovanovich.

Pring, R. (1973). Curriculum integration. In R.S. Peters (Ed.), *The philosophy of education* (pp. 123-149). London, UK: Oxford University Press.

Read, H. (1943). *Education through art.* London, U.K.: Faber & Faber.

_____. (1965). *Icon and idea.* New York, NY: Schocken.

Ridley, D. (1969). *Definitions and criteria of creativity: A literature review.* Washington, D.C.: Office of Education (DHEW). (ERIC Document Reproduction Service No. ED 108 235).

Rogers, A. (1990). Art education curriculum in British Columbia between the wars: Official prescription - unofficial interpretation (pp. 153-164). In D. Soucy & M. Stankiewicz (Eds.), *Framing the past: Essays on art education.* Reston, VA: National Art Education Association.

Rogers, C. (1961). *On becoming a person.* Boston, MA: Houghton Mifflin.

_____. (1970). Towards a theory of creativity. In P.E. Vernon (Ed.), *Creativity* (pp. 137-151). New York, NY: Penguin Books.

_____. (1982). *Freedom to learn for the eighties.* Columbus, OH: Charles E. Merrill.

Rugg, H. & Schumaker, A. (1928). *The child-centred school.* Yonkers on Hudson, NY: World Book Co.

Santayana, G. (1959). Pleasure. In M. Weitz (Ed.), *Problems in aesthetics* (pp. 637-645). New York, NY: Macmillan.

Saskatchewan Arts Education Liaison Committee. (1991). *The arts count in education.* Saskatoon, Sask.: Author.

Schactel, E. (1959). *Metamorphosis.* New York, NY: Basic Books.

Schwab, J. (1970). *The practical: A language for curriculum.* Washington, DC: National Education Association.

Shulman, L. (1987). Knowledge and teaching: Foundations of the new reform. *Harvard Educational Review, 57*(1), 1-22.

Skinner, B. (1968). *The technology of teaching.* New York, NY: Appleton-Century-Crofts.

_____. (1974). *About behaviourism.* New York, NY: Alfred A. Knopf.

_____. (1976). A behavioural model of creation. In A. Rothenberg & C.R. Hausman (Eds.), *The creativity question* (pp. 267-273). Durham, NC: Duke University Press.

Smith, A. (1992a). The art history connection: An inquiry into the connections between art history and art education. *Journal of the Canadian Society for Education through Art 23*(2), 6-11.

_____. (1992b). Copy right, copy wrong, copy cat: The legitimate imitation of images from art's history. *NSCAD Papers in Art Education, 6,* 39-46.

Smith, R. (1970). Aesthetics and humanities education. In S. Schwartz (Ed.), *Teaching the humanities* (pp. 53-69). London, UK: Macmillan.

Snider, A. (1989). Towards a personal mythology of teaching. *Canadian Review of Art Education, 16*(1), 45-51.

Soucy, D. (1989). More than a polite pursuit: Art education for women in Nova Scotia, 1887-1930s. *Art Education, 42*(2), 23-24, 37-40.

Soucy D. & Stankiewicz, M. (Eds.). (1990). *Framing the past: Essays on art education.* Reston, VA: National Art Education Association.

Spencer, H. (1860). *Education: Intellectual, moral, and physical.* New York, NY: D. Appleton.

Spencer, H. (1911). *Essays on education.* London, UK: Dent.

Sperry, R. (1968). Hemisphere disconnection and unity in conscious awareness. *American Psychologist, 23,* 723-33.

_____. (1973). Lateral specialization of cerebral function in the surgically separated hemispheres. In F.J. McGuigan & R.A. Schoonover (Eds.), *The psychophysiology of thinking* (pp. 209-229). New York, NY: Academic Press.

Stake, R. (1975). *Evaluating the arts in education.* Columbus, OH: Charles E. Merrill.

Stankiewicz, M. (1984). The eye is a nobler organ: Ruskin and american art education. *Journal of Aesthetic Education, 18*(2), 51-64.

_____. (1992). From the aesthetic movement to the arts and crafts movement. *Studies in Art Education, 33*(3), 165-173.

Taunton, M. (1986). The conveyance of aesthetic values during art activities in grades one through three. *Arts and Learning Research, 4*(1), 56-63.

Templeton, D. (1990). Developmentalism: Undo, undid, undone. *Canadian Review of Art Education, 17*(1), 29-36.

Tolstoy, L. (1959). What is art? In M. Weitz (Ed.), *Problems in aesthetics* (pp. 612-21). New York, NY: Macmillan.

Torrance, E. (1962). *Guiding creative talent.* Englewood Cliffs, N.J.: Prentice-Hall.

Van Manen, M. (1990). *Researching lived experience: Human science for an action sensitive pedagogy.* London, Ont.: Althouse Press.

_____. (1991). *The tact of teaching: The meaning of pedagogical thoughtfulness.* London, Ont.: Althouse Press.

Weltzel-Fairchild, A. (1991). Describing aesthetic experience: Describing a model. *Canadian Journal of Education, 16*(3), 267-280.

Weiss, J. (1992, April). *The muse as educator.* Paper presented at the Annual Conference of the American Educational Research Association, San Francisco, California.

Wilson, R. (1951). An operational definition of originality. *American Psychologist, 6,* 297.

■ Index